Maritime Perspectives

An Anthology
Submarines, Technology, and History

John Merrill

Sept 29, 2009

Dr Somers,
a small book for a fini Doctor

John Merrill

ISBN 0-7414-4548-4

Published by:

INFINITY
PUBLISHING.COM

1094 New DeHaven Street, Suite 100
West Conshohocken, PA 19428-2713
Info@buybooksontheweb.com
www.buybooksontheweb.com
Toll-free (877) BUY BOOK
Local Phone (610) 941-9999
Fax (610) 941-9959

Printed in the United States of America

Printed on Recycled Paper

Published April 2008

Author's Note:

As I continue to research and publish articles primarily about naval history and technology, one of my goals has been to bring some aspects of maritime history that have been covered by naval historians and others to additional audiences.

Following the my career in Navy research and development related to submarine systems, these historical monographs represent a post-career interest in exploring the history and telling the story of the development and implementation a number of submarine or submarine-related technologies. Several of the papers present a record of the creativity of some individual engineers and scientists and their contributions to the United States Navy. In most of the papers submarines provide a common thread. With some exceptions, events of the 20th Century predominate.

All the articles appeared in *The Submarine Review* the quarterly publication of the Naval Submarine League, a professional organization for submariners and submarine advocates founded in 1982. The quarterly journal provides a forum for exchange of thoughts on submarine matters. The monographs (published 2002-07) are reprinted with permission from the Naval Submarine League.

The articles selected bring to mind ***pro*** and ***anti*** submarine aspects of many of the 20th century technologies. Oceanographic knowledge and instruments such as the bathythermograph and others surely are in the *pro* category. Submarine radio communication and Loran (in its day) as a navigation aid provided support to the submarine's mission. The sea mine in concept is certainly adversarial but submarines can deliver sea mines. Sonar technology presents a dual position. On the submarine, it is a weapon for locating targets and as a tool for evading the enemy and his weapons.

Foreword

John Merrill has long provided the readers of *The Submarine Review* with a uniquely accessible view of the technology that keeps them dominate in their world of undersea warfare.

What first come to mind for many people about modern submarine technologies are the wonders of nuclear power, advanced hydrodynamics and ballistic missilery. The actual business of undersea warfare, however, is based on being able to operate in a militarily effective way in a most uncooperative environment. Above the ocean's surface, air, land and sea forces can use the atmosphere for unrestricted electromagnetic transmission and reception in communication with their cooperating forces and in their search for, and attacks on, enemy forces. Almost none of that radar or radio, of whatever type and frequency, is available to the submerged submarine. It's a different world down there and the technology required to be militarily dominant has to be developed without wide commercial civil adaptability, applied to usable hardware and constantly improved.

Normally, histories of technology have to be fairly complex in order to treat the process of invention thoroughly enough to meet academic standards, with all due regard for the formulas involved in explaining the math and physical sciences. What John Merrill has produced might be called *popular histories of undersea technologies* in order to achieve the accessibility cited above. It is not a simple task to do such rendering of complex and arcane material, but Mr. Merrill has done that in his various treatments of undersea warfare systems.

In addition to the authoring skill necessary to produce an *accessible, popular history* of the development of complex systems, the particular field of undersea warfare requires a good deal of in-place familiarity with the organizations and people involved. Not much of all this material appeared in the popular press, or even in academic treatises, at the time, consequently what historical source material does exist needs to be interpreted and expanded with research based on actual experience and personal knowledge. There are not a lot of folks around with the particular experience in this field that John Merrill built up in his professional years.

It is a pleasure, therefore, to be able to provide this brief appreciation of what Mr. Merrill has done to preserve these histories.

James C. Hay, Captain USN (Ret.)
Editor, The Submarine Review

Contents

Looking Around:

A Short History of Submarine Periscopes

Part I

Preface

After John P. Holland delivered his practical 57-foot submarine to the US Navy in April 1900, there was an immediate stronger international interest in submarines. By 1914 there were 400 submarines in 16 navies. The first United States periscope patent was granted in 1902, and periscope changes and improvements have been almost continuous since then.

Early submarine success in World War I brought important evidence of the submarine's capability. Still, acceptability of the submarine as a significant part of a navy remained in doubt in some circles. Beginning in the 1920s, the United States Navy assumed a broader and aggressive role in submarine design and construction. This led to submarines better matched to naval needs. Preparation for countering the improving submarine was lacking by all sides in the decades between the World Wars.

Operationally the submarine as an asset to the navy improved significantly during this period and prior to World War II. The fleet boat design with a *guerre de course* mission was in place. Part of the improvement included the development of a useful periscope capable of helping to protect the submarine and an essential tool for locating its targets.

The submarine accomplished much during World War II; with the nuclear submarine in the decades following World War II, submarine utilization broadened to include submarines designed for attack, deterrence, and intelligence. Multipurpose periscopes beyond optics tailored for the missions provided challenges at that time and now for periscope designers and engineers. During the entire 20th Century, the periscope changed, remaining always a key to meeting the mission needs of the submarine.

Introduction

The concept of seeing around corners with two mirrors, each mounted at the ends of a tube, predated by years the somewhat still primitive but more sophisticated optical submarine periscopes that became a routine part of all submarines by World War I.

Today, it is difficult to imagine a submarine without two periscopes. However, John Holland's successful *Holland VI*, the first practical submarine delivered to the United States Navy in April 1900 lacked a periscope. Even though elementary periscopes were extant when the 53-foot. *Holland VI* was under construction, Holland was not inclined to include a periscope in the design.

Holland's preferred way of sighting was to porpoise the submarine and note the location of the target through 3-inch by 3/4-inch plate-glass viewing ports located around the top of the turret with its 24" diameter hatch.[1] His technique of broaching, sighting the target, and then submerging like a porpoise, in lieu of a periscope for visibility and target sighting did not enhance the submarine's stealth. Several years later, improvements using prisms, lenses and other enhancements brought an improved periscope capability far beyond techniques that had been used such as the *camera Lucida*[2] while improvements have been made but the basic principle (the reflection of objects through mirrors or prisms arranged in a tube) prevailed in the 20th century. Periscopes were a necessary addition. Without a periscope, even at shallow depths the submarine was running blind underwater.

---

[1] Holland's *Fenian Ram*, launched in 1881, also had viewing ports.
[2] An 19th century prismatic device that projects an image of an object on a plane surface for tracing.

The evolution of how to build a practical submarine took many years. The advent of the more practical *Holland VI* in 1900 and the ensuing spurt in submarine construction established the need for submarine operators to know what surrounded them up on the surface but at the same time not to be seen. The optical solution was the only one available. Bringing the optical tube into the pressure hull raised overall submarine design questions as well as optical engineering issues in adapting to the submarine and its environment. The periscope tube penetration of the pressure hull and the attendant potential for water leakage provided persistent engineering demands. During the entire 20th Century, periscope-engineering goals were always present.

Origins

By the beginning of the 19th century, scientists and inventors were using mirrors and prisms to maneuver images for viewing. Yet only towards the end of the century did a submarine application for these techniques come into prominence. The 1880s saw Holland diligently moving his designs towards his ultimate submarine. In 1881, 1883, and 1885, three submarine launchings represented Holland's efforts without periscopes. At the same time, other submarine inventors and builders such as Claude Goubet in France, Thorsten Nordenfeldt in Sweden, and Stefan Drzewiecki in St. Petersburg, Russia were similarly investigating, building and selling submarines with periscope capability.

The March 16, 1916 issue of the *Scientific American* cast light on the origin of the periscope.

Who invented the Periscope?

To the editor of the Scientific American:

It is stated by some writers that the periscope, the eye of the submarine, was invented by the French. The first device of this kind to be used in naval warfare was invented by Thomas Doughty in 1864. He was at that time acting chief engineer in the U. S. Navy. During Banks's Red River expedition Doughty was on the turreted monitor *"Osage."* The gunboats were annoyed by bushwhackers and Confederate cavalry picking off their men. Doughty rigged up a sheet iron tube extending from a few feet above the deck to the engine room below, with opening near the top and bottom, and by arrangement of mirrors he could see on shore. When attacked, he would signal the gunners to turn loose, and the enemy soon learned to give the *"Osage"* a wide berth. He little realized that his invention would be utilized in the world's greatest war...He distinguished himself in the Red River expedition and subsequently at Mobile. He was one of the old-time, resourceful engineers of the Mississippi River and after the war he resumed his profession. He died in St. Louis in 1896.

W. R. Hodges
St. Louis, Mo

A contrary view to U.S. Navy engineer Doughty's 1864 Civil War periscope appeared in the Professional Notes of the Naval Institute *Proceedings* in 1914. "The development of the Submarine Boat Periscope—As an historical fact it has been set forth that a submarine boat sight tube was invented in France by Marie Davy" in 1854. Prisms as a substitute for mirrors in a periscope were reported as early as 1872.

In 1877, during the Russo-Turkish War, Drzewiecki made trials with a submarine using a propeller and equipped with periscope towers. This Polish inventor and scientist is credited with being the first to use an optical tube, the forerunner of the modern periscope. The French 118-foot submarine *Morse* included a periscope in 1899.

1900-World War I

Submarine construction flourished and in the United States, the Electric Boat Company laid down the keels for five Holland VI type submarines in the fall of 1900 and two more in 1901. In Great Britain between 1902 and 1905, Vickers Sons and Maxim constructed thirteen Holland-type submarines under Electric Boat Company patent leasing. As the first British submarine (A1), was being built, secrecy was part of the scene. British Navy personnel assigned to the submarine were designated as "for special service."[3] The actual construction was clandestine and took place undercover in a "yacht shed," The word submarine was avoided because of secrecy. Stealth as a unique attribute of submarines may have been the reason, but submarines and the word secret often go together.

Sir Howard Grubb's Periscope Patent

Captain Reginald Bacon RN, the first Inspecting Captain of Submarines and head of the embryonic British Submarine Service, saw the need for a periscope. Because of Captain Bacon's interest, Sir Howard Grubb, a well-known Irish scientist, authority on optics, and telescope manufacturer, was asked to design a periscope. Grubb's first United States periscope patent in 1901 was followed with a second United States patent in 1903 with a modification to include the use of relay optics for a wide field of view.[4]

---

[3] Richard Compton-Hall, *Submarine Boats: The Beginnings of Underwater Warfare*, Arco Publishing , NY, 1984 (p.1-3).
[4] "Notes on Submarine Periscopes," William J. Rowan, <u>Navigation</u>, Spring 1967, Vol. 14, No. 1., p. 8.

Initially the British A1[5] and A3 were fitted with short periscopes. Later, Captain Bacon as a passenger on board a periscope-equipped submarine took over command during an exercise and in the excitement of a pursuit encountered a <u>low bridge</u> with the <u>periscope up</u>. Only the periscope was damaged. Five of the first seven A1 British submarines were eventually equipped with the Grubb-designed periscope.

In February 1902, the Royal Navy cabled Isaac Rice (President of Electric Boat) "Course can be accurately kept by Sir Howard Grubb's periscope." It has been noted that Frank Cable of Electric Boat, in England at the time, brought back the idea of a periscope to the United States.[6] The United States submarine SS5 (*Moccasin*) commissioned in 1903 was periscope equipped. Five of the seven initial Electric Boat submarines were equipped with periscopes. For the next fifty years, the periscope was the submarine's only visual aid until underwater television was installed aboard the nuclear-powered submarine *Nautilus* (SSN 571) in 1954.

The Professional Notes section of the Naval Institute *Proceedings* for June 1902, disclosed "Recent reports that a new periscope permits a submarine to survey the surface from a depth of 50 feet, while formerly to a depth of 20 feet. The new periscope is telescopic." The rapid increase in the numbers of submarines may be noted in a further comment in the *Proceedings* stating that the French government ordered the construction of 13 additional submarines.

The *Fulton,* an experimental submarine launched June 12, 1902 by the Electric Boat Company, was eventually sold to Russia. It was intimated that its periscope was

---

[5] The periscope on the submarine A1 was non-rotatable. When the A1 was lost in 1904 with all hands due to a collision with SS Berwick Castle, the non-rotatable periscope may have been a cause.
[6] Compton-Hall, *op. cit.,* 1984.

useless with the submarine at 20 feet.[7] In the early days, British periscopes were stored on deck in a horizontal position. To operate the periscope, the submarine had to be on the surface; the periscope raised and secured by stays to hold it in position before diving. In the lowered position, the periscope head was sleeved in canvas. Retractable periscope masts appeared later.

Simon Lake, a Connecticut submarine inventor and builder from the Bridgeport area, constructed his first sophisticated submarine, the *Protector,* in 1902. The 65 foot 130-ton submarine included a Lake periscope patented in 1903 called the "omniscope".

With its series of lenses and prisms, it allowed the entire horizon to be viewed plus an estimate of the range to a target. Lake was the first to use a rotating periscope on a submarine. An improvement on his periscope was patented the same year and called Combined Ventilating and Observing tube." (The ventilation concept could be considered a precursor to the German "schnorkel[8] developed in the1940s.

The U. S. Navy tested Lake's periscope in 1902-03; comparing it with Grubb's British designs; and it became U.S. Navy's favored design.[9] Lake offered the *Protector* to the United States Navy. The Navy hesitated: Russia, then at war with Japan, purchased the *Protector* from Lake and ordered five more submarines from him. Later, during World War I, Lake built submarines for foreign nations as well as for the United States Navy.

---

[7] Jeffrey L. Rodengen, *The Legend of Electric Boat,* 1994, p. 49.
[8] Rowan, *op, cit.* 1967, p. 7.
[9] Both Simon Lake and Sir Howard Grubb were developing periscopes in 1902 and the Navy attributes the invention to both men. However, it was during World War I that Grubb while, responding to the demand for periscopes brought the design closer to perfection.

The *Adder*, the second A Class submarine built by Electric Boat Company and commissioned in 1903, conducted a submerged periscope trial. The periscope was rigged through the forward port ventilator. This allowed the submarine to run for three hours at a depth of 11 feet with the conning tower 7 ½ feet below the surface of the water.

The advantage of two periscopes soon became apparent: one with larger optics designed for broad area search, with smaller optics in the second periscope optimized for attack. For example, one of the Japanese Holland-type submarines launched in 1905 was equipped with a second periscope. In the 1906, the United States Navy contracted for three submarines, each equipped with two periscopes.

Water leakage and vibration were two long-term periscope-engineering problems. The leakage caused image fogging and improved periscope joints and desiccation techniques provided mitigation. Vibration degraded the performance of the optics. These deficiencies were addressed and relieved as periscopes evolved.

An abundance of names for underwater viewing instruments confronted users through the years. Names for these early periscopes included Hydroscopes, Omniscopes, Storoscopes, Cleptoscopios, Altiscopes, and Eleptoscopes. The names optic tube and periscope persisted. From 1901-1907, as many as thirteen United States patents were awarded for submarine periscopes and their improvement. Two periscope inventors patented 360° or panoramic presentation to the user. Early periscopes, even with targets presented upside down when astern and standing on their ends abeam, still allowed users to judge relative bearings.

Water leakage and vibration were two long-term periscope-engineering problems. The leakage caused image fogging and improved periscope joints and desiccation techniques provided mitigation. Vibration degraded the performance of the optics. These deficiencies were addressed and relieved as periscopes evolved.

An abundance of names for underwater viewing instruments confronted users through the years. Names for these early periscopes included Hydroscopes, Omniscopes, Storoscopes, Cleptoscopios, Altiscopes, and Eleptoscopes. The names optic tube and periscope persisted. From 1901-1907, as many as thirteen United States patents were awarded for submarine periscopes and their improvement. Two periscope inventors patented 360° or panoramic presentation to the user. Early periscopes, even with targets presented upside down when astern and standing on their ends abeam, still allowed users to judge relative bearings.

By the first decade of the 20th Century, submarines were increased in length and diameter. The tonnage expanded from the Holland's 63 tons to 160 tons with a larger crew 2 officers and 9 men instead of Holland VI crew of 7. The length increased from 63 to 105 feet; this extra length made room for a conning tower six feet above the deck, providing an improved position for navigating on the surface. The conning tower also afforded a much better housing for the periscope, now recognized as a vital part of the submarine. In some submarines having the eyepiece of the periscope located in the conning tower instead of the control room, an additional ten feet of periscope height and thus greater observation range was achieved.

It should not be inferred that periscope development or the melding of the periscope with the submarine platform was anywhere near a *fait accompli* at this time. Finding solutions to engineering problems proved difficult as a result of the periscope's operating in a troublesome salt-water environment that included mechanical stresses from movement through the water, changes in temperature, and impact on the periscope and its optical system by water wave action. Water leakage at the seal between the pressure hull and the periscope tube was a constant problem. The wake or feather made by the periscope tube at the water's surface could give away the submarine's presence. In 1910, under the aegis of the Anti-submarine Warfare Committee recognizing this weakness sponsored experimental machine gun firings at periscopes as a way to counter enemy submarines.[10] Long-term engineering addressed minimizing the periscope's wake and visibility (optical and later radar).

The long periscope tubes moving through the water vibrated and degraded the images, requiring a reduction in the speed of the submarine. This challenged submarine periscope system designers. Periscope vibration also originated from the submarine itself. It should be noted that during World War II, German U-boats were sometimes limited to speeds of less than five knots when attacking an enemy because of the effect of vibration on optical sighting.[11] For this reason, many attacks were conducted on the surface. The mechanical requirements presented by simply the raising, lowering and positioning of the periscope were enormous and required years for refinement.

Another significant aspect in this evolution relates to the submarine adapting to the operational needs of the periscope. Maintaining the periscope at a nearly constant position with respect to the height of the periscope head above the surface of the water was a formidable task for the evolving submarine. Addressing these requirements became an ongoing quest for both the Navy and those involved in the engineering and manufacture of periscopes and the design of the submarines. Some of the solutions were immediate while others awaited continuing technological advances in the years ahead.

---

[10] Brayton Harris, *The Navy Times Book of Submarines*, Berkley Books, 1997, p. 158.
[11] Michael Gannon, *Operation Drumbeat,* Harper & Rowe Publishers New York, 1990, p. 42.

While sighting with the periscope, particularly at low speeds, it was essential to keep the periscope at a fixed height above the water's surface. Holding the submarine steady within one or two feet made for difficult handling. Torpedoes also prompted submarine handling improvements. The potential for broaching and veering as the torpedo exited the submarine emphasized the need for improved handling. Later, this need for improved handling was addressed when bow planes were added to ease depth keeping and broaching. The United States E-Class submarine launched in 1912 included horizontal bow rudders or bow planes to enhance depth keeping.

Early pre-World War I periscopes typically were fixed height and mounted in a fixed-ahead position. The former required the submarine to porpoise to bring the periscope head above the surface. The fixed-ahead required the submarine to change course to look in another direction. Periscopes, which could partially extend and contract into the hull, were an improvement.

Beginning with the *USS Seal* commissioned in 1912 Simon Lake constructed 28 submarines for the Navy during the period 1910 to 1923. Simon Lake was the only competitor of John Holland and is credited with design aspects of the modern submarine including escape trunk, conning tower, diving planes, control room, and rotating and retractable periscope.

By 1912, simple periscopes and the gyroscopic compass simplified submarine navigation. About this time, retractable cable-controlled periscopes were being introduced in some submarines such as the D-Class. Optics needed improvement and lenses required frequent desiccation to prevent fogging. The new submarines were designed to keep up with the fleet, and the periscope had to be long enough to see from 30 feet below the surface.[12]

---

[12] Alden, John D., *The Fleet submarines in the U. S. Navy*, Naval Institute Press, 1979, p. 4.

World War I Begins

As mentioned above, at the start of World War I in August 1914, there were 400 submarines in 16 of the world's navies. Innovations and improvements abounded and effective submarine use as an offensive weapon was slowly beginning to be recognized. By 1914, submarine speed was about 14 knots on the surface and 9 knots submerged. The submarine's stealth, improving agility, and better Whitehead, Bliss-Leavitt, and other torpedoes plus the periscope contributed to greater acceptance of the submarine as an implement of war. Total acceptance of the submarine was gradual for other reasons. The submarine, not in the capital ship class, was considered as the weapon of the weaker nation; its full potential was not universally grasped.

Acoustic sensing at this time was in a primitive stage of development during World War I; this proved to be a two-edged sword. The submerged submarine's presence was not as likely to be determined by the searching enemy. Antisubmarine warfare, including weapons such as depth charges to destroy enemy submarines, was in a rudimentary stage. On the other hand, without an acoustic sensing capability, the submarine submerged was deaf and blind when operating below periscope depth. The propellers of nearby surface ships could sometimes be heard in the submarine.

The submarine was handicapped at periscope depth; the distance to the horizon for sighting targets was minimal because of the periscope closeness to the surface of the water. Even surfaced with a raised periscope, the submarine's range of vision in clear weather was less than the range of vision of an enemy target or submarine hunting surface ship much higher above the surface. A 1915 book on submarines noted that a periscope 20 feet above the water could observe a battleship at 10,000 yards and 2,200 yards at 1 foot. Submarine-hunting aircraft with their ability quickly to search wide areas of ocean were soon recognized as an additional liability for submarines on both sides.

Longer periscopes allow the submarine to observe at a greater depth but introduce other problems. In addition to increased water pressure, a longer optical tube is more prone to vibration from water action. Increased length causes image dimming due to the greater optical length. The September 2, 1914 issue of the *Scientific American* reported treating lenses with magnesium fluoride to reduce dimming. Increasing submarine diameter accommodated longer periscopes, increasing height of the upper periscope lens above sea level. This lengthened the distance to the horizon, although not significantly.

Antisubmarine hunting aircraft benefited greatly due to their height of observation and the distance to the horizon. During World War I, an aircraft at 5000 feet could sweep an area of about 300 miles. This improved; and in World War II, aircraft were responsible for more than half of the 800 U-boat sinkings. The aircraft is assisted further by the wake created by the periscope head as it moves through the surface of the water. Wake reduction was eventually achieved by narrowing the upper portion of the periscope tube to have a pencil-like shape. Periscope heads with dimensions a few inches or less were achieved in some instances. U-boats by 1918 were generally fitted with "altiscopes," which enabled them to look for aircraft in the area before surfacing. In the latter part of World War I, convoys accompanied by aircraft were virtually immune from U-boats.

Dr. Frederick Kollmorgen

Born in Germany in 1871, following university studies Dr. Kollmorgen directed his career to optical instrumentation and lens development. Before coming to the United States in 1905 to work at the Keufel and Esser Company in New Jersey, he held positions as an optical advisor with telescope manufacturers in Austria and England. In 1909, he made application for his first submarine periscope patent, which was granted October 11, 1911. These basic optical elements and mechanical structural designs pioneered by Kollmorgen continued in use throughout the 20th Century.

In 1916, when World War I stopped imports of foreign lenses and optical instruments, Kollmorgen headed a small group of scientists and technicians that formed the Kollmorgen Optical Corporation in Brooklyn, New York. Their purpose was to design and build periscopes for the expanding submarine service of the United States Navy. For the remainder of the 20th Century, the Kollmorgen name has been associated with numerous state-of-the-art U.S. Navy submarine periscopes and those of other navies.

A recollection by George Carroll Dyer (Vice Admiral, USN, retired) is of interest. In 1919, Dyer was the commanding officer of a Holland designed D-Class submarine.[13] The Electric Boat Company (EBCO) constructed the three D-Class submarines in 1909-1910. D-Class improvements cited by EBCO included having two periscopes. Dyer recalls operating with a fixed position periscope:

"The D-3 had a fixed periscope, which meant that you had to be on an absolute level in order to really make a

---

[13] The British version of the D class approved in 1906 were the first to be diesel driven and fitted with a gun.

decent approach on a target. Because if it got the least bit angled down by the stern, which the D-3 was very apt to do, you couldn't see anything except the sky. Because the periscope was fixed. It was the last class of submarines that had the fixed periscope. All the rest had eyepieces that could be elevated or depressed. If the submarine got a little angled down, you turned the glass up. "[14]

Scientific American Supplement No. 2055, May 25, 1915 in "Various forms of the Periscope" reported on the principles and development of a valuable instrument used in war. The section on submarine periscopes provides a summary of the state of the art at that time.

The general characteristics point out that modern periscopes (1915) have a length of from 16 to 24 feet, and a diameter of 6 to 9 inches, field of view of about 65 degrees and a magnification of 1.25 to1.5. The optical system can be rotated to face in any required direction and the eyepiece remains fixed.

The article included components of the periscopes built by Sir Howard Grubb, the primary provider for the British Navy:

1. A reversed telescope, giving a reduction of about 0.25

2. A telescope giving a magnification of about 2.0

3. An erecting prism which can be rotated so that the image given by the system is correctly oriented

4. A telescope giving a magnification of 3.0

The two telescopes (1&2) were face to face, first reducing the image and then enlarging it. The last telescope

---

[14] U.S. Naval Institute, Oral History Collections

(4) included a fixed eyepiece and prism, so arranged that the observer looks horizontally at the object. At the focus of the eyepiece are placed a scale and pointer to show the bearing of the object sighted and a ruling to allow the distance to be estimated when the size of the object is known.

Periscope advances included photography. In 1915 between May and December, a British E Class submarine (Holland design), using a periscope equipped with a camera in the Sea of Marmora, penetrated Constantinople harbor and took photographs.

Periscope Status 1917

A 1917 book by Marley F. Hay, *"Secrets of the Submarine"*, summarizes the periscope and some its characteristics at that time. The author credits French submarines with having periscopes 50 years previously (1867). He generalizes that all submarines have two periscopes and some three. Vertical observation of aircraft is the primary use of the third. With diameters of six inches most scopes can be set at 18 or 20 feet above the superstructure deck with the top of the scope 3 or 4 feet above the surface of the water in a moderate sea. The top five or six feet are tapered down to two or three inches in diameter and painted in mottled colors to obscure the periscope. In some instances, a dummy seagull is mounted on top to provide further camouflage. Periscope viewing arranged in the conning tower and in the control room is typical. Other periscope features include horizon scan with a field of vision of 40° - 60°, a rotating upper prism to provide images in correct positions, and magnifications of the order of 1-4.

Gyroscope Compass

Elmer Sperry's gyroscope compass (patented in 1908) was installed on the submarines E-1 and E-2 commissioned in early 1912. Prior to this invention, only non- ferrous magnetic material could be used for periscope construction. Further, when submerged the magnetic compass did not function well in the steel hull as the magnetic compass was surrounded by electromagnetic fields produced by the electric propulsion motors. The compass was mounted outside the hull and viewed with mirrors or a telescope from the conning tower. In general use of magnetic materials in the vicinity of the compass was minimized where feasible.

Kollmorgen Begins

During the World War I period, Bausch & Lomb, Keuffel and Esser, General Ordnance and the newly founded Kollmorgen Optical Company comprised the sources of U. S. Navy submarine periscopes. The improving submarine platform required periscopes having proper magnification, field of vision, vertical and horizontal movement and other attributes that would optimize the ability of the operator to assess his environment.

Addressing these requirements under a 1916 contract with the Chief of the Department of Construction and Repair, Kollmorgen delivered his two original periscopes (one forward and one aft), to the K-l (SS-32). The submarine, commissioned in 1914, was 154 feet long, displaced 521 tons, and was one of the twenty U.S. submarines to reach the war zone and report for duty in the

Irish Sea and near the Azores. The Navy paid Kollmorgen $1,385 and $1,685 for the periscopes.[15]

Periscope Disguise

In November 1917, the War Department received a recommendation from a lawyer in Oakland, California, with a suggestion to make the periscope above the water less conspicuous: Disguise the periscope with a decoy of a bird with a glass breast and wings movable by springs. Additional decoys of birds native to the geographical area could provide and make the periscope-mounted decoy a less likely target.

Periscope Assessment

That periscopes were yet to be perfected can be seen in an accounting of periscope problems faced by the fleet of 27 R-Class boats constructed during World War I. Problems included poor focus, lack of eye cushions on the ocular or eyepieces, low power, air bubbles and moisture leaks into the inner tube, lens scratches, leaks, missing screws, and hydro-dynamically induced vibration at normal submerged speeds.[16]

War Reparations: U-boats

At the end of WWI, six German U-boats were made available to the US Navy at Harwich, England, as part of war reparations. They were brought back to the United States. The Navy's operational forces carefully examined the U-

---

[15] *The Submarine Periscope 1916-1991*, Kollmorgen Corporation, Northampton, MA, (no date) p. 6.
[16] Periscope comments from *Building American Submarines, 1914-1940,* Gary E. Weir, Naval Historical Center, Department of the Navy Washington D.C. 1991. p. 77.

boats' capabilities. As a result, the following years were sometimes referred to as the "German Years." These German submarines influenced the designs of new United States submarines into the 1930s. The Chief of Naval Operations (CNO) created a list of private contractors and subcontractors who were allowed to examine the technological advances presented by the U-boats. Kollmorgen, by 1920 an important periscope builder, was included in this CNO list of companies allowed to go aboard and examine the German advances in submarine design and construction.

Between the Wars

In the 1920s, the aforementioned Navy examination of German submarines strongly confirmed the potential for improvement in United States submarine design and construction. Additionally with the experience of building more then 70 submarines during the World War I period, the Navy perceived a need to control the contractors. To achieve this, the Navy began an expanded and more direct role concerning submarines and their procurement. The goal of improving the quality of the United States submarine diesel engines, radio communication capability, periscopes, armament, habitability, and other factors led the Navy to take this step. The contractor, not the Navy, drove submarine technology at this time. Acting in the new role of coordinator and catalyst for the first time, Kollmorgen, Sperry Gyroscope Company, Electric Boat Company, and others were supported by the Navy to advance submarine technology.

For the following fifteen years, an ongoing debate regarding the mission of the submarine continued, hampering a consensus regarding the Navy's submarine needs. The mission choices debated included coastal defense, battle-fleet support, fleet independent operations using stealth to advantage, independent offensive operation, and unrestricted warfare policy. This indecisiveness defining the submarine's role led to a variety of submarine designs prior to the mid-1930s fleet submarine configuration which prevailed during the entire World War II and accommodated the role of unrestricted warfare. This fleet boat design emulated the successful U-boats and warfare of Germany's World War II *course de guerre*. German submarine designs such as the U-135, one of the World War I reparation submarines, provided a reliable prototype for submarine design.

These years saw the Navy more actively and broadly participating in the design and engineering of submarines. Moving away from dependence on commercial submarine builders, the Portsmouth Navy Yard became an important center for submarine engineering development and construction.[17] Between the years 1914-1971, 134 submarines were constructed at Portsmouth. It has been stated that in the pre-nuclear, era more submarines were built at Portsmouth than any other yard. By the mid-1930s, Mare Island Naval Shipyard in California was added to the Navy's active submarine building program.

In related technical fields, radio communications, underwater sound, and periscopes (Kollmorgen) were given Navy support and encouragement. Advances in these technical areas took place during this period at government, industrial and university locations.[18] With Navy assistance, Kollmorgen's financial and management practices were improved and their periscopes were widely installed.

German U-boat periscopes were found to be superior to those found on British or American submarines. For example, the periscope heads tapered to less than inch in diameter and provided a reduced and more difficult target at sea level. It was clear that American optics needed upgrading. Improvements followed, but the quality of the 1918 German U-boat periscope still exceeded that of United States periscopes. Quality United States periscopes were available by the late 1930s.

---

[17] Richard E. Winslow III, *Portsmouth Built: Submarines of the Portsmouth Naval Shipyard,* Portsmouth Marine Society Publication Six, Published by Peter E. Randall Publisher, 1985.
[18] Gary E. Weir, "Silent Defense 1900-1940," Undersea Warfare/Summer, 1999, p 14.

Barr and Stroud Ltd. of Glasgow, Scotland, periscope builders, discussed in their 1922 pamphlet "The Submarine Periscope" the technical aspects of their state-of-the- art periscopes which consisted of cruising or lookout (surveying the horizon), attack (conning the target), and night scopes. The article pointed out the light loss in a periscope amounting to as much as 31% due to the optics.[19] Sky search capability, desiccating apparatus, pressure capability of the order of 100 pounds per square inch, a range and inclination finder, and velocity of a target were cited as features of importance for submarine periscopes.

The March 1927 issue of the Naval Institute *Proceedings* cited a Japanese periscope development. Trials aboard the Japanese submarine B-16 included satisfactory testing of a periscope enlarging six diameters, which made it possible to see correctly as high up as 1,000 meters.

Bureau of Construction and Repair (BCR)

Charged with ship construction, including periscopes, Bureau personnel responsible for periscopes were sometimes perceived as reticent in regard to change. A 1983 book on submarines commented on the BCR "...and they fought change every step of the way... That change came at all was through the pushing tactics of the young submarine commanders—who had to live with the product."[20]

In the post World War I period, the BCR moved toward the standardization of type and design of periscopes. The goal was to improve periscope replacement and parts supply. Previous to 1927, contracts for submarines covered

---

[19] The light loss in a single polished lens can be about 4%. Some coatings may reduce the loss to -½ % to -¼ %. Without coatings only 5% of the available light would reach the eyepiece.

[20] Edwin P. Hoyt, Submarines at War: History of the American Silent Service, Stein and Day, NY, 1983, p 68

the entire boat, installation and equipment. As a result, there were 70 different periscopes, all similar with the same essential features. This precluded interchangeability and made replacement and parts supply difficult. As a step toward resolving this difficulty, a Manual of Instructions for Submarine Periscopes was issued. The manual included detailed drawings and specifications from four manufacturers.

US Navy Periscope Builders 1927	
Company	Periscopes in the Fleet[21]
Bausch & Lomb Optical Co. New York, NY	80
Kelvin, Bottomly & Baird Glasgow, Scotland	10
Keuffel & Esser Co. New York, NY	50
Kollmorgen Optical Co. Brooklyn, NY	136

---

[21] These periscopes were raised and lowered using cable hoists and motors. In mid-1944, the *Spikefish* (USS 404) recently launched was the first to be fitted with hydraulic periscope hoists.

United States submarines increased in length and beam beginning in the mid-1920s to 1930s.

Class	Length	Beam	Year
Barracuda	341'	27' 7"	1924
Argonaut	381'	33' 10"	1928
Narwhal	371'	33' 3"	1930
Dolphin	319'	27' 11"	1932
Cachalot	271'	24' 9"	1933

Periscope Length [22]

1916	10-20 feet
1945	30
1960	30-40
1990	46

Typically 40 or 50 feet longer with greater beam than earlier submarines, the new dimensions made it possible to have longer periscopes. The longer periscope tubes required greater rigidity to prevent excessive vibration causing poor images and possible damage to the optics. At that time, existing tubes were constructed of brass, naval bronze, or composites, and low speed was required to reduce vibration. German periscope tubes constructed of steel were found to be more rigid, less susceptible to vibration problems and had experienced little corrosive action due to seawater. Steel became the material of choice for periscope tubes by many

---

[22] Operating in shallow water with a long periscope can be a challenge.

of the world's navies. Periscope bending due to movement through the water was countered by using two tubes: an outer one to resist pressure and an inner to contain the telescopic components.

Periscope Stadimeter

A stadimeter is a device for determining the range to an object of known height. Measuring the angle between the horizon and top of the object (usually the masthead) whose height is generally known provides a basis for the range calculation. The range is independent of the angle of that target to the submarine. By mid-1928, the Navy was evaluating stadimeters. One was a United States Naval Gun Factory type Mark V stadimeter with a range of 8000 yards. The other, made in Jena, Austria by the Carl Zeiss Company, had a range of 11,000 yards and was of particular interest. Models were placed aboard the three V-Class submarines for evaluation. The 1930s saw periscopes equipped with stadimeters. In addition to its use in fire control, the stadimeter became useful in both piloting and navigation via the periscope.

Three Periscopes

The mine-laying 381 ft. *USS Argonaut* (SS166), commissioned in 1928 at Portsmouth, was the largest submarine built by the United States until after World War II and was equipped with three periscopes. Two were raised and lowered by cable hoists, the eyepiece of one in the conning tower and one in the control room. To reduce vibration, the upper periscope was equipped with a streamlined retractable section (fairing). The other scope in the conning tower was raised and lowered hydraulically. Later, it was determined that this periscope was not needed and it was removed.

Through the years, two persistent periscope problems confronted engineers. Previously mentioned, one was vibration of the scope tube as it passed through the water. The other was related to the exposed periscope head and the wake or plume of the above- water portion of the periscope as a target. The former was addressed by providing a fairing to streamline the part of the tube exposed to the water. A fairing may reduce vibration at speeds of 6-7 knots or higher. Decreasing the target size was addressed by tapering the upper section of the tube and minimizing the size of the head to reduce the observed wake of the above-water portion of the periscope. Camouflaging the exposed section was also implemented.

No. 725,839.   PATENTED APR. 21, 1903.
                              H. GRUBB.
APPARATUS FOR FACILITATING THE SIGHTING OF DISTANT OBJECTS
          FROM SUBMARINE BOATS, BARBETTES, &c.
                     APPLICATION FILED DEC. 13, 1901.
NO MODEL.   3 SHEETS—SHEET 1.

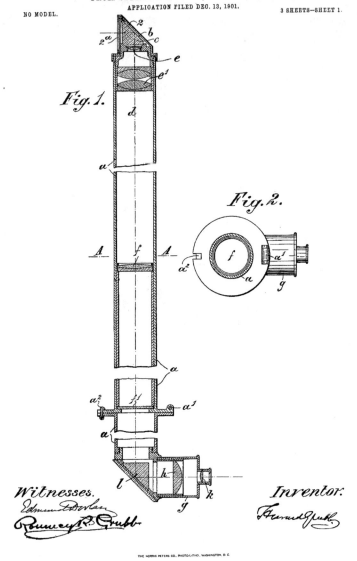

Fig. 1.

Fig. 2.

Witnesses.   Inventor.

Sir Howard Grubb's Periscope Patent

Lowering periscopes to East 32nd Street, Manhattan, in front of the Kollmorgen plant in 1916.

Courtesy Kollmorgen

1,006,230.

Patented Oct. 17, 1911.

3 SHEETS—SHEET 2.

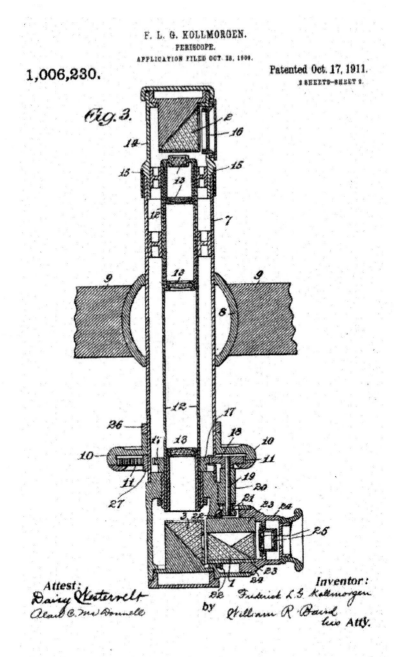

Fig. 3.

Kollmorgen's First Submarine Periscope Patent

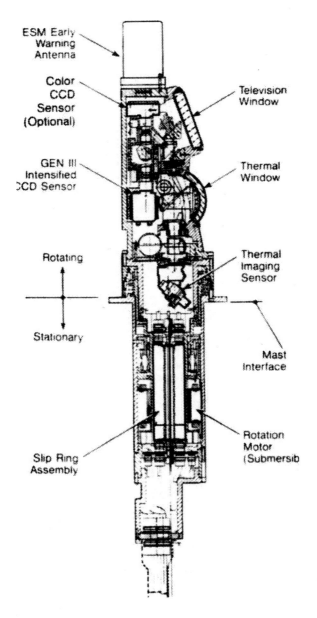

ESM Early Warning Antenna

Color CCD Sensor (Optional)

GEN III Intensified CCD Sensor

Rotating

Stationary

Slip Ring Assembly

Television Window

Thermal Window

Thermal Imaging Sensor

Mast Interface

Rotation Motor (Submersib

**Electro-Optical
Non-Hull Penetrating Periscope**

Looking Around

A Short History of Submarine Periscopes

Part II

World War II

The Ubiquitous Periscope

The periscope is omnipresent throughout <u>Sink 'em all: Submarine Warfare in the Pacific</u>, Vice-Admiral Charles A. Lockwood's factually accurate and technically correct (as credited by Fleet Admiral Chester W. Nimitz) account of the United States submarine in the Pacific in World War II. Throughout the book, a typical recurring quote regarding a submarine attack read "up periscope; and stand by number one tube" or an equivalent comment concerning the periscope.

More than 200 submarines meeting fleet boat capabilities were constructed between 1941 and 1945. The Balao Class *USS Bowfin* (SS287), commissioned May 1, 1943, was typical of the wartime fleet type submarine at 311 feet in length, crew of 80, 20 knots surfaced, 10 knots submerged, 1,526 tones surfaced, and a 75-day cruise capability.

Like most other submarines of the period, the *Bowfin* carried two periscopes. The one nearest the bow, designated as No. 1, was the night scope and with a large head providing the highest usable light-gathering power and a large 7mm-diameter exit pupil. The length of this periscope was 36 feet with a net weight of 2000 pounds. The No. 2 aft periscope was the attack scope with a tapered upper section and small diameter, 2-½-inch head leaving a smaller wake or feather in the water from the periscope to be seen. The narrower design also reduced light transmission and the diameter of the exit pupil (4 or 5mm). The attack scope was four feet longer and had about the same weight as the night periscope. Kollmorgen manufactured both *Bowfin* periscopes. The periscopes were equipped with a stadimeter for measuring the distance to an object of known height.

By 1927, as noted previously, Kollmorgen dominated the United States periscope field. At the Kollmorgen plant in Brooklyn New York, the1944 wartime production rate of USN submarine periscopes peaked at one periscope per day. The typical World War II periscope cost $10,000 and by the mid-1950s the price became $30,000. Multiple functions and operation at increased depths and speeds accounts for some of the price change.

Type 2 Daylight Attack Periscope

The Type 2 daylight attack periscope was introduced into the submarine fleet in 1942 and found wide use and acceptance during World War II and in the decades following. It is recalled today (2001) with great respect for its superb optics by some present day submarine personnel who operated with the Type 2. The optical capability of more recent periscopes with a variety of non-optical devices crammed into the coveted space is not held by some with the same regard.

The periscope's long slim neck (1.4 inches in diameter) with a very small head resulting in reduced wake made it attractive for use in submerged daylight attack operation. In the post World War II era, modifications were made to provide greater pressure capability (greater depth). Other changes in later models included improved optics, optical coatings, and photo capability. In particular, reduced photographic vignetting effect was achieved with better optical elements.

A Japanese Horse Race Track

The USS *Guardfish* (SS217), commissioned May 8, 1942, was on its first war patrol by August off the coast of Japan close to Yagi, a port in Northern Honshu. The city's horse race track could be seen through the periscope. Photographs taken with the periscope supported the memory of the event and proof that the viewing took place. This frequently-cited incident is evidence of the then-current periscope's optical and photographic capability as well as the courage of the submarine and its crew. It is notable that on this initial patrol, the submarine was credited with sinking 70,000 tons of enemy ships.

Off Tokyo Bay

The *USS Jack* (SS259), a fleet submarine commissioned in January 1943, in Groton, Connecticut, was on its first patrol off Tokyo Bay by mid-June. The new submarine sank more than 16,000 tons of Japanese merchant shipping on this patrol. Admiral James F. Calvert in Silent Running: My Years on a WWII Attack Submarine recalls the role and some of the use of the periscope. Concerning the sighting of targets: he writes "Our routine was to expose about two feet of scope. With that height we could see the tops of an average maru's masts at maybe three or four miles. This meant that the circle of our observation was only six to eight miles in diameter, an area of about fifty square miles at best." Target hunting with a periscope was a formidable task. A further use of the periscope concerned the presence of enemy aircraft: "...the remaining thing the OOD had to be careful about with his periscope watch was the presence of aircraft...They were hard but not impossible to see through a periscope."

Type 4 Periscope with Radar

A meeting of submarine officers and logistics planners in December of 1943 at Mare Island concurred that the performance of a new night periscope would be enhanced if a radar antenna (providing active detecting and ranging) and electronics could be squeezed into a standard 7 ½-inch periscope tube along with the optics. ComSubPac Admiral Lockwood was a participant. A 9-inch diameter night periscope, in use by some foreign navies, would more easily accommodate radar and was considered. However, the larger diameter increased the threat to the submarine's stealth in the event that it was needed in a daytime emergency. Development of the new periscope moved ahead. The 7 ½-inch diameter Kollmorgen radar-equipped periscope was tested seven months later on the newly-commissioned *Sea Fox* (SS402).

In November 1944, the Kollmorgen Type 4 periscope including the new ST firing range radar, augmenting the on board SJ radar, was operational on the *Spikefish* (SS 404), a Balao Class 400-foot operating depth submarine. This submarine was also the first to be fitted with hydraulic periscope hoists replacing the cable and motor arrangement.[23]

With the ST radar and the periscope in the same mast, a radar approach to a target and the periscope approach became simultaneous, with attendant advantages. The Navy's submarines in the Pacific did not overlook this benefit. In combination, the ST and SJ radar provided targeting improvement at night and during conditions of fog. In an emergency, this could be used for daytime approaches. The pairing could also work against radar-equipped Japanese escorts.

Further, this periscope was the first to introduce navigation by periscope and a reasonable photographic capability.[24] In the years ahead, use of the mast for multiple functions increased. The companion periscope, the Kollmorgen Type 2 (attack periscope) developed during the 1930s, was widely installed in the fleet type submarine of WWII and continued in extensive use as late as the 1990s. As previously mentioned, its features included a narrow 1.4-inch diameter neck, and enhanced optics for daytime use. The Type 4 complemented the Type 2 for night submarine torpedo attacks. As the war ended, Kollmorgen had two general categories of periscopes: the Attack (Type 2) and the All-Purpose (Type 4).

British Periscope Length

With regard to periscope length, military historian Peter Padfield noted that British submarines were at a disadvantage in an attack during World War II because their periscopes were shorter. They were made of bronze, so as not to affect the magnetic compass in the conning tower. Other navies were using steel. Bronze (unable to bear the length that steel could support) resulted in a loss of periscope depth of 10 to 16 feet. "British boats were more subject to surface swell, hence more difficult to control and more liable to break surface at critical moments in an attack."[25] Padfield points out that the conning tower (also constructed of bronze) added weight that was compensated for by using thinner plating for the pressure hull. This reduced submarine diving depth. German and United States hull plating was three-quarters to seventh-eighths inches thick while British plating was slightly over half an inch.

German Periscope Innovation

On the first day of World War II September 3, 1939, the U-30 sank the Atlantic liner *Athenia* by torpedo 250 miles northwest of Northern Ireland. The toll in lives was 112 including 28 Americans. The liner was en route from

Glasgow to Montreal with primarily refugees as passengers. The sinking was contrary to German rules of engagement at that time and caused an international stir similar to the sinking of the liner *Lusitania* in 1915. Padfield cited above in War beneath the Sea recreated the torpedoing. Concerning the periscope, "...he [Commanding Officer Oberleutnant Fritz-Julius Lemp] swung himself on to the metal bicycle-type seat straddling the attack periscope housing abaft the hatch opening. Unlike the system in other navies, the eyepiece on the German attack periscopes did not move up or down with the shaft but remained at a fixed height..."[26]From his seat, the operator's right hand controlled the height of the scope and the left, the focus and stadimeter.[27] The any-height periscope capability later was a feature of a 1950s Kollmorgen Type 6 attack periscope.

U-boat Periscope Conditions for Attack

In The U-Boat Commander's Handbook,[28] attack instructions highlight the periscope's role under favorable and unfavorable circumstances. Even under favorable conditions, cautions and limitations must be observed, including minimizing periscope height. Sea states 2 to 3 and wind levels of 3 to 4 are favorable. However, if the sea is as smooth as oil, "The slightest ripple even of the low periscope is noticeable, and easily observable by the enemy. Exceptions: enemy coming out of a bright sun; conditions of twilight; moonlit nights."

Post World War II

Periscopes and the Nuclear Submarine

With the launching of the first true submersible, the nuclear-powered USS Nautilus (SSN 571) commissioned September 30, 1954, two factors heavily influencing periscope specifications for the remainder of the 20th century involved the depths and speed of the nuclear submarines. The greater underwater speeds available with the advent of nuclear power demanded a periscope capable of being raised at high speed without vibration damage. As operational depths, increased watertight integrity became a prime consideration to be met by the periscope builders with heavier periscope tubes and improved pressure seals.

Periscopes under the ice[29]

In 1957, during the initial under- ice probe for a nuclear submarine the *Nautilus* (SSN 571) came within 180 miles of the North Pole. This investigative trip by the first nuclear submarine introduced a new role for the periscope. Under some conditions, a view aided by sunlight of the underside of the ice could be seen. For some situations a topside floodlight was available. But sonar remained the primary tool for under ice navigating.

During the early part of the trip to the ice shelf, the Number 1 periscope, with a badly-packed hull fitting, dripped seawater leakage on the user. Once repaired, both scopes became useful later when skirting under the ice. However, while proceeding slowly under ice in a northerly direction, periscope casualties of a serious nature took place. A polynya appearing to be free of ice was not. As the Nautilus gradually moved up toward the surface of the polynya, the Number 1 scope went black. The periscope was bent and could not retract because it was bent. Number 2 periscope was damaged beyond repair. Skill, effort, and clever stainless steel welding in an Arctic environment brought the Number 1 periscope back to operability. Periscopes are helpful but not absolutely vital under ice. Sonar is essential.

Missions and Surveillance

The Cold War development of the strategic fleet ballistic missile submarine with its pivotal deterrent role and unique mission needs created further significant demands on periscope design and engineering creativity. In particular, the precise navigation needed for missile launch led to the development of the Kollmorgen Type 11 "Star Tracker periscope." This periscope developed for the Polaris submarine is capable of taking automatic star sights to allow the submarine to determine and maintain its position with an accuracy of seconds of arc.

At the same time, new and varied intelligence and surveillance missions of some attack submarines brought about additional fresh periscope requirements. The periscope tube and head as real estate was highly sought. Expanded portions of the electromagnetic spectrum vied for space. Optical (visual, photographic, navigation, and laser), infrared (imaging), and electronic warfare support measures (ESM) antennas contended for room in the periscope head and tube. With severe space limitations, challenges abounded. The periscope engineers and builders and the engineers and scientists of the other periscope electromagnetic systems at government and industrial activities found the requirements particularly demanding. The post-war periscopes with the multiple capabilities may best be described as "all-purpose periscopes."

In the 1950s, a common periscope need was how to improve bundling the various non-optical systems in the limited diameter (7 ½-inch) periscope tube. The Navy's goal was to develop and enhance the other systems sharing the space with the optics including photographic, electronic surveillance measures antennas, radar, and sextant navigation. A further objective involved improving the mechanical aspects of operating the periscope. The Kollmorgen Type 8B, delivered in 1959 and widely installed in the United States submarines, incorporated some of the aforementioned features and also included a new electric motor to quietly and easily train the periscope in azimuth.

The Periscope Builders

Throughout the last half of the 20th century, the Kollmorgen Corporation remained the primary, developer, integrator, and builder of submarine periscopes for the U.S. Navy. In 1952, the U.S. Navy moved the company from Brooklyn, New York to Northampton, Massachusetts.

During the 1950s, the U. S. Navy decided it was necessary to have at least two sources of supply for all critical systems on the submarine. In addition, it was expedient to foster competition. The U. S. Navy funded Kollmorgen to transfer periscope- manufacturing know-how to Sperry Marine in Charlottesville, Virginia. This was a successful effort; and even though Kollmorgen maintained its stature as the developer of periscopes, Sperry successfully competed with Kollmorgen into the early 1990s. Bausch and Lomb in Rochester, New York also had a brief involvement during the 1950s in the building of submarine periscopes.

Periscopes representative of the 20th Century are shown in Figure 1. A significant number were designed, manufactured, and delivered by the Kollmorgen Company. The periscopes addressed solutions to new submarine mission requirements, new submarine speed and depth capabilities, and the implementation of technological innovations. Some of the modifications or changes were optical; others related to the various systems co-located in the periscopes and produced by other companies.

Kollmorgen improvements during the 1950s included photographic instrument enhancements and the inclusion of the first radar detection system. Advanced optical coatings were introduced at this time, significantly reducing the reflection losses in the optical elements. To increase the length of a periscope in some designs, typically Kollmorgen uses three relaying telescope sets. For these periscopes with as many as 30 optical elements with 60 surfaces, light loss reduction is essential.

In general, each periscope stems from a previous design. The World War II Type 4 all-purpose periscope evolved in 1951 into the Type 8 with a navigation capability incorporating a tilting head prism. Initially, this was due to longer submerged periods as a result of the snorkel. The extended undersea capability of the nuclear submarine required further celestial navigation improvement using the periscope. The Types 9 and 10 were developed to answer this requirement. Both were versions of the Type 8. A program in 1957 adding a communications capability emerged as another version of the Type 8 with a 7½-inch tube and replaced the Types 9 and 10. This Type 8B with increased edge illumination from 10% to 40% for photography was in the fleet by 1959. More recently, the Type 8B has been further modified to incorporate additional satellite communication capability.

Navy Laboratory Role in Submarine Periscopes

At the Navy's Underwater Sound Laboratory (USL) at Fort Trumbull in New London, Connecticut, optical and electro-optical systems investigations began in 1947 with the development of infrared detectors for use on surface ships. The Laboratory's submarine antenna group experience included periscope antennas.

As alluded to earlier, by the mid-1960s, a consensus within the submarine community was converging on three submarine missions attack, deterrence, and intelligence. Periscopes appropriate for each mission share common attributes but the different missions have unique needs. Solutions to the equipment needs for the various systems embedded in the periscope were found in the advanced technology available in such areas as photography. Adapting the technology to the periscope and submarine environment required resourcefulness. Designing for and implementing the new periscope requirements broadened Navy periscope Research and Development participation. It was at this juncture that USL's participation in the Navy's periscope programs changed significantly.

**New London Laboratory
Administrative Designations**

USL merged with the Naval Underwater Weapons Research and Engineering Station at Newport, Rhode Island July 1, 1970 to form the Naval Underwater Systems Center (**NUSC**). In January 1992, NUSC was disestablished and succeeded by the Naval Undersea Warfare Center (**NUWC**) Division Newport. Navy base closures during the 1990s resulted in the transfer of the New London Laboratory personnel to the Newport location.

The Navy solicited including Perkin Elmer, ITEK, and Kollmorgen industry for proposals. Kollmorgen and the ITEK Company in the Boston area were awarded "winner takes all" prototype development contracts. Kollmorgen eventually won the competition and continues to produce and improve the Type 18 today.

In 1967, the Washington projects office responsible for "reconnaissance, electronic warfare, special operations, and naval intelligence processing " (REWSON) and aware of USL's submarine interests and ability to address optical and electro-optical research and engineering problems brought the Laboratory into the Type 18 development program. This engineering advisory role for the Laboratory occurred after the start of construction of the demonstration Type 18 periscopes. State-of-the-art optics in the new periscopes was the primary emphasis. Periscope work placed new demands on the Laboratory's physicists, electrical, and mechanical engineers through generations of periscopes, including the current non-penetrating periscopes.

This new assignment took place as the periscope was continuing to evolve from simple optics-only systems used for visual observation into more complex systems incorporating communications, radar and ESM countermeasure antennas, and eventually satellite communication capability. Equipment to support visual observation such as TV and photographic cameras were add-on devices and not universally readily available at that time.

Kollmorgen and ITEK, both Massachusetts companies were competing for the Type 18, each constructed a demonstration periscope (optics) for evaluation at sea. Based on the sea tests and evaluations, USL made recommendations regarding the details of the planned periscope that included increased light-gathering capability, image motion compensation, stabilization, and enhanced photographic capability. Kollmorgen won the competition for the full-scale development of the Type 18 periscope.

REWSON assigned NUSC to oversee the full development, installation, and test and evaluation of the new Type 18 periscope. A particular area of attention by the New London Laboratory was integration of the TV and photographic aspects of the new periscope. Successful completion of Technical and Operational Evaluations at sea of the Type 18 followed in 1971 and 1972.

Initial employment consideration for the Type 18 involved a modest production of systems as mission requirements dictated. It soon became evident that the SSN 637 Class and the growing SSN 688 Class submarines could benefit from the special capabilities of the Type 18 on all missions. Further, the 1972 production contract with Kollmorgen included a complete design of the ESM portion of the system, since the original demonstration model of the Type 18 provided optics only. The New London Laboratory was tasked to oversee the Type 18 production and fleet introduction. The initial production periscope installation was performed on board the USS Cavalla (SSN 684) by a NUSC/Kollmorgen team in mid-1975.

By 1981, Kollmorgen manufactured 52 Type 18 periscopes. Three years later, the New London Laboratory developed significant Type 18 periscope documentation based on the New London Laboratory's intense involvement with installation and introduction of more than 40 Type 18 periscopes on SSN 637 and 688 Class submarines. The total production of the 688-Class was more than 60 submarines. This documentation allowed the fleet to maintain, repair and support the periscope's logistics. It was the first submarine periscope brought under Navy configuration management.

As the various periscopes developed, the Laboratory's technical involvement and contributions included areas such as electronic imaging and introduction of satellite capabilities for communications, and navigation including the satellite Global Positioning System (GPS).

During the 1978-80 time frame, NUSC received further periscope development work under the sponsorship of the Office of Naval Intelligence (ONI). A new mission oriented periscope, the Type 22 (a replacement for the Type 16) was developed for the SSN 688 and SSN 637 Class submarines. Both the Types 16 and 22 were designed and manufactured by Sperry Marine at Charlottesville, Virginia. These periscopes were used as mounting devices for deploying imaging systems, and both used basic Type 2 unique optics. NUSC Type 22 responsibilities included sensor integration, maintenance and installation. Periscope building by Sperry Marine began in 1955. In 1995, Kollmorgen purchased their product lines.

Periscope Facilities

In the mid-1970s, the increasing periscope role at the New London Laboratory resulted in the construction of a periscope facility at that location in order to be able to conduct periscope work. It was determined that requirements and specifications for such a facility did not exist. Subsequently, a specification and design for a periscope facility was developed at New London. A facility was constructed and opened in December 1977. The facility was expanded in 1984 to accommodate periscope satellite systems. In 1985, the Laboratory developed a Naval Sea Systems Command guide for periscope facility development and provided assistance in the improvement or construction of new periscope facilities in Hawaii and at the Trident Submarine Bases at Bangor, Washington, and Kings Bay, Georgia.

Trident Periscope

In 1974, NAVSEA selected NUSC as their technical representative agent for the development of the Trident Fleet Ballistic Missile Submarine periscope shipset. The periscopes that were developed by Kollmorgen for Trident were modifications of the Type 15 and Type 8 periscopes. The Trident periscopes are the US Navy's longest periscopes. Both periscopes function as optical instruments and antenna masts, and include omnidirectional or direction-finding antennas for signal reception in support of early warning, and contain antennas for external communication and satellite navigation.

In 1979, an early Trident ship set was delivered to NUSC for a yearlong test program. Trident Ohio class periscopes were the first periscopes developed from a full Navy specification and the first to have integrated logistics support as a fundamental consideration in the development.

Periscope Systems Engineering at NUWC

Beginning in 1992, NUWC undertook technical initiatives with financial support from the intelligence community that improved overall periscope performance for mission requirements. This was accomplished by engineering the most advanced imagining and sensing capability (exclusive of the optics) into a Kollmorgen Type 18 periscope.

Commercially available high-end technology devices appropriate to the periscope's requirements were examined, tested and engineered to accommodate the space and conditions found in the periscope. Initial success of this approach lcd to ongoing efforts for upgrading the sensors and taking advantage of the latest available devices. Principal areas include low light level color television; low light level black and white television, and the digital still camera. Significantly, the digital camera removes the need for wet photographic processing on board the submarine. Further, these new capabilities developed by NUWC are in keeping with the concept of a workstation for observation and distribution of the data collected by periscope sensors in lieu of the eye-box and the one-person observer.

The New Century

With more countries acquiring submarines, demand for periscopes continues and among the builders Kollmorgen in the United States and Zeiss (Germany) stand out. Pilkington (Barr and Stroud) in Great Britain and SAGEM (France) also produce periscopes for the current world market.

As recently as June 2001, Kollmorgen's venerable 1950s Type 8 periscope is cited. The news release by the Naval Sea Systems Command's Naval Undersea Warfare Center (NUWC) Division in Newport, Rhode Island identified a multimillion-dollar contract modification to incorporate infrared imaging capability into a variant of the U.S. Navy's still popular Type 8 (Type 8 Mod 3).

A Russian company (LOMO), located in St. Petersburg site of the founding of the Russian Navy 300 years ago, and a builder of periscopes for all Russian nuclear submarines, is presently developing and manufacturing an attack periscope. Features include a night vision channel, laser range finder and satellite navigation and warning antennas. The periscope is designed for prospective diesel submarines of the Amur Class.

Non-Hull Penetrating Periscopes (NPP)

For almost a century, the traditional submarine periscope remained basically the same. The NPP concept, with new image sensing initiated by Kollmorgen as early as 1978, is moving towards fruition in the new century. The technology making it possible electronically to deliver the periscope images into the submarine (control room) is referred to as optronic or photonic. These techniques make NPP possible.

The NPP by not requiring a 5-10 inch diameter periscope mast to penetrate the submarine hull enhances hull integrity. In addition there are more opportunities for periscope location. The periscope may be entirely located in the submarine's sail (fin). With fiber optic and wire data transmission, the new telescoping mast eliminates the deep well and the nearly fifty feet of hull-penetrating optics tubes that are installed on current generation submarines. NPP allows greater flexibility in submarine hull design, as it is not necessary for the periscope mast to be directly above the submarine's bridge, also allowing a more optimal use of space. It has been commented that in the future the optical periscope is still likely to continue as the choice for some submarine configurations.

Electro-Optical Periscope

In 1992, a Kollmorgen prototype optronic hybrid system using commercial visible and infrared spectrum cameras was built under a contract with the Defense Advanced Research Projects Agency (DARPA) and demonstrated for sixteen months on the *USS Memphis* (SSN 691) a Los Angeles Class submarine. Currently Kollmorgen, Pilkington, and Zeiss are producing versions of NPP.

Kollmorgen's Optronic Mast includes features like ESM, communications, and GPS antennas, color charge coupled device camera, high definition TV camera, eye-safe laser range finder, and thermal imaging camera. Pilkington's NPP mast for early 21st Century British submarines similarly contains a surveillance package that includes color, low light, and thermal imaging television cameras.

NPP technologies allow the periscope observations to be taken quickly and recorded with images later replayed, enlarged and examined while at depth by any crew member at various locations on other systems in the submarine.

Microwave direction-finding functions and other features are in the NPP. In 2001, the Virginia Class submarine and the Royal Navy's Astute Class will not include traditional periscopes in deference to two NPP systems.

A 1995 article in conclusion notes a considerable degree of customer resistance to the optronic mast at that time. "The sophistication of the sensors and their supporting electronics as well as hydraulics have raised fears about their reliability."[30] The author goes on to point out that if the optronics fail some navies are of the opinion that the submarine commander will need a periscope optical path for reserve.

Submarine Periscopes and their Customers

By the end of the 20th century, thirty countries include the submarine as a proven important component of their modern navies. Underwater imaging of the surface above the submarine is essential. Whether in the form of the now old optical path device with a variety of technological devices sharing the tube real estate or the *looking around* device (optronic) outside the pressure hull being very high technology, the "periscope" has an ubiquitous and continuing presence on all submarines.

Argentina	Ecuador	Italy	Singapore
Australia	France	Japan	South Korea
Brazil	Germany	Netherlands	Sweden
Chile	Great Britain	North Korea	Taiwan
China	India	Norway	United States
Columbia	Indonesia	Pakistan	Venezuela
Denmark	Iran	Peru	
Egypt	Israel	Russia	

Ahead

At first, the periscope task was to capture quickly and covertly the visual part of the electromagnetic spectrum. The last half of the 20th Century saw other parts of the electromagnetic spectrum sharing the periscope tube. Now, that the NPP has removed the optical link and wires, wave-guide and fiber optics are the pathways. Periscopes and their subsystems continue as the central point for surveillance, electronic warfare and intelligence gathering and with the ability to process, distribute and share information. Ahead lies the challenge of remote surveillance for the submarine in the water and above.

Periscope Summary

NOTE: Types 2,8,15,18 are Kollmorgen designed periscopes, manufacturing at Kollmorgen and Sperry Marine. Types 16 and 22 were designed and manufactured by Sperry Marine.

Type 2	(1942)	1.4 inch head, Daylight attack submerged operation
Type 2A		Improved optics, post WWII fleet periscopes
Type 2D	(1959)	2.4 inch head, advanced optical design and optical coatings (30 optical elements, 60 optical surfaces), reduced vignetting improved photographic quality, deeper submergence capability
Type 3		Celestial navigation capability
Type 4		Night attack periscope (all purpose), ST radar, navigation, photographic equipped World War II, continued use post War
Type 5A	(1950s)	Improved photographic instrument
Type 6	(1951)	Improved mast rotation mast raised and lowered with stationary eyepiece (constant optical length) servo train and elevation from a stationary console
Type 8		(refinement of **Type 4**), radio communications, electronic surveillance measures systems, celestial navigation, photographic, radar
Type 8A	(1957)	communications demonstration
Type 8B	(1959)	all purpose, electric motor for azimuth training (*USS Triton* (SSRN586) circumnavigation)
Type 9		Stabilized line –of- sight optics, sextant altitude-setting unit
Type 10		**Type 8** with photoelectric sextant, Kollmorgen continuous automatic star tracking (including unique artificial horizon)
Type 11	(1960s)	Precise sextant to support the FBM inertial navigation system.
Type 14		Attack scope with greater pressure capability than **Type 2D**
Type 15		All purpose, improved **Type 8B,** counter measures capability with improved optics and electronics)
Type 16		Special purpose to suit specific missions
Type 18	(1968)	Optimum photographic, multifunction search periscope, straight optical capability, low light operating mode, TV camera, film or electronic cameras
Type 22		Mission oriented optical and electronic periscope, special mission replacement Type 2 (superceded the Type 16)

Endnotes

[23] Richard E. Winslow III, op. cit.,

[24] Kollmorgen Corporation, *op. cit.*, p.14

[25] Peter Padfield, *War Beneath the Sea: Submarine Conflict during World War II*, John Wiley and Sons, Inc., 1995, p. 23.

[26] *Ibid.* p. 3.

[27] Harry Cooper, "U-2513 Remembered by LCDR M.T. Graham, USN (ret.)", The Submarine Review, July 2001, p. 87

[28] The U-Boat Commander's Handbook, Thomas Publication Gettysburg, PA p. 42.

[29] Comdr. William R. Anderson U.S. N. with Clay Blair Jr., *Nautilus 90 North,* The World Publishing, Cleveland and New York, 1959, p 85-89.

[30] "Periscopes and optronic masts," Maritime Defence, Vol. 20, No. 7, March 1995, p. 36-38.

Acknowledgment

Curator Stephen Finnegan and archivist Wendy Gulley at the Nautilus Submarine Force Library and Museum in Groton, Connecticut, made periscope archival material available which was most valuable concerning the early part of the 20th Century.

A great number of people, who really knew and understood periscopes, came forward and patiently helped me unravel the history of the periscopes of the last half of the 1900s. These physicists and engineers (primarily with careers at USL, NUSC, and NUWC) included John Comiskey, James Flatley, Carl Floyd, Gary Motin, Ralph Polley, Herman Ruhlman, and Paul Sheldick. Roger Densmore of Analysis and Technology Inc. provided further historical details. Herbert E. Torberg, a long time Kollmorgen engineer, scientist and company president greatly increased my understanding of periscopes. Douglas Jones, Matthew Richi and John Nixon of Kollmorgen provided significant additional insight.

Depth Charge:

An Early Antisubmarine Warfare Weapon*

Part I

*The monograph is primarily about the depth charge its beginnings and the years of World War I. Post War years saw little development of the weapon. The paper concludes with a brief comment regarding the depth charge at the beginning of World War II and the direction of depth charge developments during the War years.

World War I Opening Days

As World War I began, the German U-boat, initially encumbered with existing rules concerning visits and searches of intended targets, was assumed to be an inefficient war weapon. Rules of engagement for the U-boats were limited by the difficult Prize Regulations governing submarine actions against nonmilitary vessels established by eight nations in the 1909 London Declaration. The Regulations were designed to protect neutral nations' maritime rights and international seaborne commerce in the event of War.**

During these early months of the War, the 1909 agreement significantly hindered effective submarine aggression. 'The alternative to sink noncombatants vessels without warning struck prewar sensibilities as so barbarous that in January 1914 Britain's First Lord of the Admiralty, Winston Churchill scorned the idea that a civilized power would ever adopt such a policy."[1] Germany was challenged for the next several years with following the Prize Regulations or departing from their use and adopting unrestricted submarine warfare. By early 1917, three years later, it was the latter. These years of indecision resulted in fewer U-boats and little technological advance in their submarines.[2] During these early years of the War, the United States negative view of unrestricted submarine warfare was a significant factor in curtailing Germany's use of submarines. According to E. B. Potter, throughout the first U-boat

----

**Many of the Declaration's submarine inhibiting operational restrictions regarding the sinking of merchant ships were echoed later in the London Prize Ordnance protocol agreement just prior to World War II in November 1936. Germany and England were signatories. The restricted/unrestricted warfare role for the submarine was again in play during the early part of WW I

campaign from February 22, 1915 to September 20, 1915, the U-boats held back because of the possibility of United States entry into the war.[3]

At first, the small number and size of German submarines also reduced assessment of the potential threat. Some of the German submarines were less than 100 feet long with a crew of 14. Germany's naval intentions in the early stages of the War were directed toward Britain's Grand Fleet. The German U-boats were relegated to the role of reconnaissance and torpedo support for the German High Sea Fleet in dealing with the Grand Fleet.[4] The torpedo as a submarine weapon, although available in small numbers early in the war, was not in general use until March 1917. Prior to that time most sinkings by U-boats were by gunfire.

At first, both sides overestimated the military capabilities of their enemies. Consideration of enemy submarines as potential targets was not in the purview of the designers of the existing destroyers and torpedo boats and their weapons. As submarine warfare developed, it became a close and comparative intimate encounter of a few hundred yards between enemies while the standard range of engagement for the grand fleets took place at 20,000 yards. A new type of warfare required new tactics and weapons. It turned out that all through the War, the U-boat sea keeping and endurance did exceed expectations.

First Sinkings by U-boats

With few exceptions such as First Sea Lord Sir John Fisher, the menace of the submarine was initially disregarded. On September 5, 1914 a month and a day from the start of the War, U-21 sank the Royal Navy light cruiser *Pathfinder* with one torpedo. A blockade was quickly established with more than eighteen cruisers. On September 22, the German U-9 torpedoed and sunk blockade patrol

British heavy cruisers *Aboukir, Hogue*, and *Cressy*. Six weeks into the war, a war zone was in operation with an Admiralty heavy cruiser blockade of the entire North Sea and the waters between Iceland and the Norwegian coast.

These events and later on the increasing and extraordinary loss of merchant shipping from the unrestricted sinkings coming from adoption of a *guerre de course* strategy by German U-boats pushed the Allies to accelerate development and implementation of antisubmarine weapons to attack and sink the German submarines. As observed by Admiral John Jellicoe of the Admiralty commented in 1920, British antisubmarine measures were almost nonexistent at the beginning of the war.

Throughout the War antisubmarine weapons improvements followed but the development by scientists and engineers of effective ways to detect submerged submarines did not begin to emerge until the latter part of the War and then only in rudimentary form. The primary Allies' tactic against the U-boat during the first several years of the War was an offensive approach to search, find and destroy. In large oceans and no practical way to locate the enemy submarine, the success rate was low.

World War I U-boat Classes

Class	Range/Speed miles /knots	Max Depth (feet)	Length (feet)	Crew
U Long range cruiser	11220/8 surfaced 56/5 submerged	164	230	39
UB I Coastal	1650/5 45/4	164	92	14
torpedo attack	9040/6	246	180	34
UB III	55/4			
UC Coastal mine layer	750/5 55/4	164	110	14

Not long into the War the Royal Navy met with success in blockading the German High Sea Fleet. Lacking capital warships to confront the British but with U-boat prevailing against merchant shipping, the German and Central powers confined their naval effort almost completely to submarines. It was not until mid-1917 that the Allies initiated broad merchant ship convoying essentially defeating the *guerre de course* efforts by German submarines. The Allies Antisubmarine Warfare forces (air and sea) included the depth charge in their armament.

Available Weapons

Initially the tools at hand for countering submarines were drift and stationary nets, mines, deck guns and ramming. Mines were widely used but it has been pointed out that as of January 1917, the British did not possess a mine that was satisfactory against submarines.[5] However, a new mine based on a German design developed by the Admiralty was in place and effective against the U-boats by November 1917. A surfaced submarine could be rammed. During the War nineteen U-boats were sunk in this way. Merchant ships also rammed and sunk five U-boats. "As time went on, all the later destroyers were fitted with steel rams at the bottom of the stem, and very efficacious they were as tin-openers"[6]

Damaging or sinking U-boats by shelling was not effective because it was difficult to hit such a small target with normal low freeboard before it dived. In addition, with intensive submarine crew training the number of seconds required to dive gradually decreased, thereby giving surface ship gun crews less time to hit the target. With regard to diving times during World War I, times ranged from 20 seconds to one minute.[7] In 1917, the latter part of the war, U-boat dive times were of the order of 40-45 seconds and by 1918, 30 seconds.[8]

When submarines first started firing torpedoes, ships attempted to use a high-speed zigzagging strategy to avoid being hit. As the speed of submarines improved, ships resorted to other methods. Light steel nets were hung around warships beneath the water line to deflect incoming torpedoes. These nets were ineffective and were soon removed from warships.

Improved skill with the periscope and better submarine construction over time allowed the submarine to be first in becoming aware of its surface enemy and to frequently escape or take aggressive action. A target must be visible for gunfire to be effective. The submarine's stealth improved. The Royal Navy invoked submarine versus submarine, and eighteen U-boats were torpedoed and destroyed.

Towed explosive sweep was also examined to determine if it would be an effective antisubmarine tool. After testing, the method was found to be inadequate for reasons that included the safety of the pursuing vessel's equipment handling crew. Another antisubmarine weapon-- the lance bomb a hand thrown 7-pound charge contact weapon--proved to be ineffectual even though used in great numbers (20,000) by 1917.[9]

Early antisubmarine efforts by mid September 1914 included the deployment of 250 trawlers and drifters (a boat fitted for drift-net fishing) to support Royal Navy U-boat hunting in spite of the lack of adequate weaponry if armed. Their role included sweeping mines, antisubmarine patrols and watch for German mine layers. Eventually, auxiliary antisubmarine support vessels included whalers, trawlers, motor launches, motorboats, tugs, yachts, minesweepers, and paddle wheel boats.

British Auxiliary Patrol Vessels[10]

January 1915	827
January 1916	2595
January 1918	3301

Antisubmarine Weapons

The U-boat losses cited in the tables below are at some variance. However, the overall effectiveness of the antisubmarine arsenal through the World War I years is demonstrated.

U-boat Losses [11]

	1914-16	1917	1918	Total
Depth charge	**2**	**6**	**22**	**30**
Gunfire	10	6	4	20
Mines (inc. German)	13	26	19	58
Ramming	3	10	6	19
Sweep	2	0	1	3
Torpedo (inc. German)	6	7	7	20

Against the U-Boat 1914-November 1918 [12]

Weapon	Class of Ship	Destroyed	Damage Serious	Damage Slight
Depth Charge	Man-of-War	-	6	3
Depth Charge	Destroyers and Patrols	35	85	182

In March 1915, the depth and lance bombs were considered in the experimental stage but by August large orders were placed for depth charges. Slow production created limited availability in 1916. However, damage to the

U-boats began with direct or indirect U-boat sinkings from depth charges.

By the end of World War I, the antisubmarine warfare tools included the hydrophone for detection of submerged submarines, the 300 pound TNT-or Amatol-filled depth charge, and mines. These weapons plus the mid-1917 implementation of merchant ship convoying met with success against the U-boats.[13] Placing mines at various depths along busy sea-routes also dealt with the U-boats. Estimates of high as high as 75 U-Boats destroyed have been made. Minefields also blockaded hostile submarine bases. The depth charge, a primitive concept, was eventually adopted by most of the Allies and enemies. "The depth charge was the original dedicated ASW weapon."[14] Airplanes and blimps with depth charges were also added to the enemy submarine hunters.

Antisubmarine weapons and tactics brought to fruition during 1914-1917 included the depth charge that improved the performance of Naval ships and other support vessels and aircraft in their increased and effective escort role for the merchant ship convoys that began in the spring of 1917. The depth charge was prevalent among supporting naval vessels. Requirement for large numbers of depth charges is seen in the number of ships involved in a typical convoy. A convoy of 10-50 merchant ships escort consisted of 1 cruiser, 6 destroyers, 11-armed trawlers, and 2 torpedo boats each will aerial balloon.[15] Depth charges were important weapons for the supporting ships as well as the merchant ships.

Regarding aircraft, dirigible airships and airplanes had important ASW roles. During 1917, airplanes sighted 185 U-boats and attacked 85. Airships located 26 U-boats and attacked 15. Even the then embryonic underwater detection systems to locate enemy submarines provided a modicum of advantage for the user. As 1917 ended, U-boats turned to conducting attacks in the night, whereas during the earlier years daytime attack was the *modus operandi.*[16]

John Terraine in *The U-Boat Wars: 1916-1945* places the depth charge in its historical context "… the weapon that would shortly dominate anti-submarine warfare, and become primary in World War II: the depth charge." In 1980, J. R. Hill in *Antisubmarine Warfare* echoes Terraine with "While neither as accurate nor as lethal as expected, the depth charge was still the main killing weapon of World War 2."[17]

Attacking underwater

Underwater bomb explosions to damage enemy shipping received significant attention as a weapon soon after the opening days of World War I. The submarine a technological advance required new counter measures. In the case of the underwater bomb, the above mentioned success of the U-boats in sinking naval vessels as well as merchant shipping created an instant need for some method of countering the German submarines.

Depth charge (underwater bomb) quickly evolved in Great Britain, Germany, France, and Italy at about the same time and the weapon and its implementation gradually improved. The concept was to provide a way to damage the enemy submarine that did not require contact with the target. The depth charge and the compressive forces of the water in the vicinity of the underwater explosion could damage at a distance from the target. For the next thirty years, the device continued as one of the important tools for antisubmarine warfare (ASW).

Use of exploding powder charges underwater to damage enemy naval vessels and shipping saw increased activity during most of the 19th century. In 1843, American revolver-inventor Samuel Colt and others in Europe independently proposed an electrically command-detonating of explosives under water. Colt's concept of a submarine battery did not receive government support to proceed. In the early years of the Civil War, Confederate Navy Commander Matthew Fontaine Maury (formerly USN and an outstanding nautical scientist of the 19th century) with others successfully initiated electrical triggering underwater explosives to destroy Union naval and merchant shipping underwater. This technique was successful and has been credited more than any other weapon for damaging or sinking Union naval vessels during the entire Civil War. Whitehead's 1860s epic invention, the modern torpedo, became the major undersea weapon by the end of WW II. After successful use of the depth charge during the War the status of the depth charge changed, "The US abandoned depth charges after World War II, preferring torpedos and ahead-thrown proximity contact weapons."[18]

Addressing a Need

In Great Britain, the original idea of a "dropping mine" or depth bomb dates to 1911. How to combat the new naval warfare weapons submarines and aircraft slowly emerged. In a 2002 historical paper, "Anglo-American Naval Inventors 1890-1914", speaking to the invention of the depth charge, the author said "The history of the depth charge is still mysterious." Admiral Jellicoe referring to the origins of the depth charge regarding the real inventor said "No man in particular,...It came into existence almost spontaneously, in response to a pressing need."[19]

However, several Royal Navy Officers at about the same time during 1914 perceived that a depth bomb type weapon could be used to counter the submarine. Officers cited are Admiral Percy Scott, Admiral Sir Charles Madden, and Captain P. H. Colomb. Further, Royal Navy Commander in Chief, Sir George Callaghan in October 1914 asked for a depth charge. Development started in November.[20]

Early Depth Charges (Surface and Air)

Admiral Percy Scott a long time Royal Navy technical innovator of improved naval gunnery director and range finding systems recognized the impact that submarines and aircraft would have on naval warfare prior to the start of WWI. Late in the fall of 1914, he was appointed head of the Anti-Submarine Department of the Admiralty. Scott designed a bomb that could be dropped by ships on a submarine if it was on or near the surface. He suggested that aircraft could also drop charges. Scott's advocacy also included the opinion that depth charges could be thrown from ships.

At first, depth charges were triggered using a float and a lanyard of fixed length sometimes, referred to as float and line. These English and German depth charges used the float and line for detonation in the early designs. Failure to explode was frequent.

Initial United States Navy Bureau of Ordinance depth charge designs immediately prior to entry World War I in April 1917 also used the float and line technique. In October 1914, Captain P. H., Colomb and Admiral Sir Charles Madden independently developed a depth bomb actuated by a hydrostatic valve adjusted to explode at a preset depth. It has been noted that Colomb's and Madden's schemes were sent to Scott but were somehow delayed.

British Depth Charge Status

Depth charge work started December 1914 with four primitive models including an aerial model. The following December, eight depth charge configurations were issued or

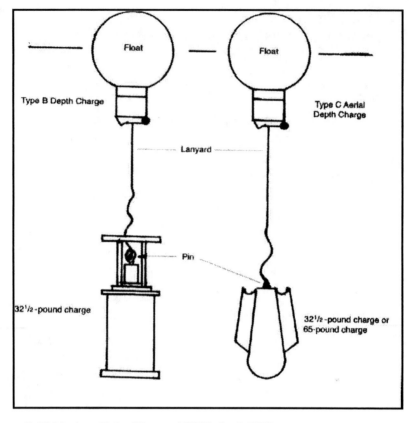

D. W. Messimer, Find and Destroy: ASW Warfare in WWI,
Naval Institute, Annapolis, MD 2001.

Float and Lanyard Depth Charge

under development in England.[21] As the depth charge was essentially a proximity weapon and the location of the enemy submarine underwater was imprecise many depth charges were required for success. Having a sufficient number of depth charges at hand was an unending problem for the remainder of World War I. Early charges used gun cotton as the explosive. Gradually, later models used TNT or Amatol as the explosive of choice, with Amatol used primarily by the British to conserve TNT. Quantities of these explosives varied from 32 to 35 pounds in the early models up to 250 and 300 pound charges later. Typical firing depth settings were in the 40 to 80 foot range. As mentioned previously, the hydrostatic valve for triggering the explosive eventually replaced the mechanical triggering devices of the earlier charges.

A 1915 British designed and developed depth charge designated Type D met with success. However, production only gradually increased. The canister (18 inches in diameter and 28 inches long, similar to a fifty-five gallon oil drum) contained either 120 or 300 pounds of TNT with a dropping rate in water of 6 feet per second. Because of its shape and size, the depth charges took on the name "ash cans."

The hydrostatic pistol or detonator was inside a hollow chamber in the middle of the depth charge and fired when the chamber filled with water. The inlet for the seawater to the chamber could be switched with a tool to six holes of different size, smaller holes causing firing at greater depths (100 to 600 feet). This was an improvement over the float and lanyard technique but with limitations. It should be noted that later in 1917 soon after the United States joined the Allies, an engineer of the United States Bureau of Ordnance after examining the British design invented and patented an improved detonating mechanism. Further comments regarding this are discussed below.

The Type D became a prototype for other improvements and adaptations. Twenty-eight years later in 1943 in World War II, it was still standing the test of time as an important weapon. In the ten months from August 1942 to May 1943, of 150 U-boat sinking, 120 resulted from the depth charge (about 85%).[22]

Depth charges typically kept in racks on the stern of the vessel could be released from the bridge and rolled overboard. A weapon in the water behind the ship presented a problem. If the ship's speed was too slow and the depth charge set for a shallow depth the danger of an early explosion was significant.

The nature of this uncomplicated way of introducing the weapon into the water behind the ship presented a problem. Upon locating an enemy submarine, the usual practice was to drop a series of depth charges at intervals of 10 or 15 second depending upon the destroyer's speed.[23] The attacking ship's speed required that it not be in harm's way when the explosion took place. Fast ships used the Type D with a 300-pound charge; slower vessels D* with a 120-pound charge. Depth charges with adjustable depth setting and greater depth capability allowed either fast or slow vessels to use the 300-pound charges.

Some Royal Navy antisubmarine vessels were equipped with as few as two depth charges in early 1916 and four charges by the end of the year. The allotment for some old destroyers was one depth charge. Depth charges also became included as part of the armament of the Allies merchant ships along with deck guns. Production numbers for the last half of 1917 show a depth charge production of 140/week in July, 500/week in October and 7800/week in December. By early 1918, a destroyer's allotment increased to 30 to 40. Success with depth charges comes about with a saturation approach therefore large numbers are required.[24] One weapon source during the period 1914-18, the Standard Ironworks located in Colchester, England, manufactured 20,000 depth charges.

Depth Charge Throwers

Early experience with the depth charge developed a new requirement. An enemy submarine by turning perpendicular to the pursuing vessel's track and increasing speed might evade and escape. This created a need to be capable of "throwing" a depth charge along a perpendicular to the centerline of the ship to widen the attack pattern by providing a type of barrage. Coupled with the stern dropped charges the throwers completed a semicircular pattern. During the War, two throwers evolved the British K-gun and the American Y-gun. In parallel with the introduction of the K-gun in July 1917 and its 75yard range, the Howitzer (a direct hit-projecting weapon with a range of 1200 to 2600 yards) became available at that time. The depth charges are a proximity weapon. These weapons introduced late in the war and in small quantity proved effective and were the vanguard of highly effective World War II depth charge throwing or projecting systems (throwing ahead) such as Hedgehog, Squid, and Mousetrap.

British K-gun

The thrower or projector, a type of mortar, was at sea by mid-1917 but, like the basic depth charge, was in short supply. The above mentioned Standard Ironworks manufactured 264 depth charge throwers (projectors) capable of handling 300 and 400 pound loads, between September and the end of November in 1917. In mid-1917, roughly 300 depth charge throwers were delivered to the Royal Navy.

The basic design of the K-gun was the Thornycroft single barrel design fitted with an arbor or stem. A standard British depth charge was secured to the stem's outer end by lashings or adjustable clips. Throwers were mounted in pairs with one set on each side of the ship, and firing was either manual by percussion or electrically by remote control from the bridge. Initially, the total weight of the depth charge and the firing stem to which it was attached was large and overall awkward to handle restricting the K-gun rate of fire. Later improvements in weapon handling and delivery to the gun overcame this limitation. By 1918, a destroyer equipped with four K-guns and stern racks could drop a pattern of depth charges to bracket the presumed position of a U-boat.

Y-gun

In 1917, the United States Navy Bureau of Ordnance was provided with photographs and designs of the Thornycroft depth-charge thrower. Considerations included the design of a gun that would reduce the impact of recoil on smaller vessels and easier to produce than the K-gun. Suitability for destroyer installation was an additional criterion. The General Ordnance Company of Groton, Connecticut made the calculations needed for the working design and undertook the production and test of the first gun. The order was placed with the New London Ship & Engine Company a manufacturer of submarine engines located in Groton.

A gun was devised to simultaneously throw two depth charges, one to port and one to starboard. The Y-gun with its simultaneous delivery of depth charges resolved the recoil problem of the single thrower. The gun shaped like a Y consisted of two barrels at an angle of 45° from the vertical capable of throwing two 300-pound depth charges. Ranges of 50, 66, and 80 yards made it possible to have a wide pattern barrage. Interestingly, on destroyers and submarine chasers the Y-gun required a limited commodity-a centerline location competing with deck guns for coveted space.

General Ordnance Company received a contract for the Y-gun December 8, 1917 and because of preliminary work in November, deliveries were made December 10, 1917. As a result of this contract, 947 Y-guns were installed on destroyers and submarine chasers.

National Ordnance Activities, p 98

Thornycroft K-gun Destroyer Quarter Deck
Depth Charges on Rack aft

Naval Institute

Mark I Destroyer Depth Charge Rack
(World War I)

Navy Ordnance Activities WWI, p104

US Navy Depth Charge Y-Gun

Endnotes

[1] Jack Sweetman, *The Great Admirals: Command at Sea 1587-1945*, Naval Institute Press, Annapolis, Maryland, 1997, p. 356.

[2] Dwight R. Messimer, *Find and Destroy: Antisubmarine Warfare in World War I*, Naval Institute Press, 2001, p. xv.

[3] E. B. Potter, editor, *Sea Power: a Naval History*, Prentice Hall, Englewood Cliffs, NJ, 1960, p. 455

[4] Karl Doenitz, Admiral, *Memoirs*, World Publishing Company, Cleveland and New York, 1959, p. 11,12

[5] Sir John Jellicoe, Admiral, *The Crisis of the Naval War*, Cassell & Co. Ltd., NY, 1920, p. 50.

[6] Taprell Dorling, *Taffrail: Being an Account of the Destroyers, Flotilla Leaders, Torpedo-boats and Patrol Boats in the Great War*, Hodder and Stoughton, Limited, London, 1931, p. 289.

[7] William S. Sims, *The Victory at Sea*, Doubleday, Page and Company, NY, 920, p. 97.

[8] John Terraine, *The U-Boat Wars: 1916-1945*, G. P. Putnam's Sons, NY, 1989, p. 27.

[9] Jellicoe, *op. cit.*, p. 56.

[10] V. E. Tarrant, *The U-Boat Offensive: 1914-1915*, Naval Institute Press, Annapolis, MD, 1989, p. 17.

[11] Robert M. Grant, *U-Boats Destroyed: The Effect of Antisubmarine Warfare 1914-1918*, Charles Scribner's Sons, NY, 1971, p. 159.

[12] *Introduction of the Depth Charge into the RN*, http://www.ku.edu/~kansite/ww_one/naval/br 1669.htm, p. 2.

[13] Philip K. Lundeberg, *Undersea Warfare and Allied Strategy in World War 1, Part II: 1916-1918*, Smithsonian Journal of History, Volume 1, No. 4, Winter 1966.

[14] www.dmna.state.ny.us/slater,. p.1.

[15] Martin Gilbert, *T he First World War:; A Complete History*, Henry Holt and Company, NY, 1994, p.329.

[16] Jellicoe, *op. cit.* p. 98.

[17] J. R. Hill, *Antisubmarine Warfare,* 2nd edition, Naval Institute Press, Annapolis, Maryland, 1989.

[18] http//www.ussslater.orge/weapons/dpthchrg.html p.1.

[19] Sims, *op. cit.*, p.94.

[20] www.ku.edu/-kansite/ww_one/naval/br 1669.htm, p. 1

[21] Jellicoe, *op. cit.*, p. 76.

[22] V. E. Tarrant, *The U-Boat Offensive 1914-1945*, Naval Institute Press, Annapolis, Maryland, 1989, p.117-119 (interpretation)

[23] US Navy, *Navy Ordnance Activities: World War 1917-1918*, p. 106.

[24] Jellicoe, *op. cit.*, p. 51, 60.

Depth Charge:

An Early Antisubmarine Warfare Weapon

Part II

World War I

Depth Charge Effectiveness

With the depth charge, the intention is to use the incompressibility of water to set off an explosion at depth in the vicinity of the enemy submarine and to create a substantial force to damage or destroy the submarine. A significant consideration is that during World War 1 once the enemy submarine submerged it was lost to the pursuer as underwater detection using sound was still in an embryo stage of development. Even as World War I ended, underwater detection of a U-boat was a low probability.

Dropping the charge where the enemy submarine was thought to be was certainly a step in the right direction for antisubmarine warfare. However the ability to achieve the goal of destroying the U-boat depended upon a number of variables. The amount of explosive in the depth charge, the depth setting for the explosive and the actual proximity of the submarine target to the event were significant factors. Success always required multiple depth charges and prior to 1918, depth charges were a scarce weapon. Nonetheless, even an exploding depth charge even without damage to the submarine could be sufficient to rid the area of an enemy submarine.

A variety of distances have been given regarding the separation required for the depth charge explosion to do damage to the target submarine. Admiral Sir John Jellicoe in 1920 recalled a 300 pound depth charge within 14 feet of a submarine hull created serious damage or sinking, and at 28 feet the submarine was disabled sufficiently to force the submarine to surface and be exposed to other weapons.[25] Precise distance requirements are difficult to define as the variables are not easily assessed. However, it is interesting that a distance for serious damage to a submarine of 25 feet was identified regarding World War I while a World War II distance of within 23 feet has been cited. Confirming these numbers, a 1993 comment regarding depth charge effectiveness in World War I stated "An underwater explosion twenty-five feet from a U-boat could destroy it and one as near as fifty feet could seriously damage it."[26] Even with an explosion not sinking the submarine, shock waves from the depth charge impacted the submarine's hull and instrumentation requiring some submarines to immediately surface. On the surface ramming or gunfire could be effective. Admiral Jellicoe referring to the impact of the depth charge noted "...at distances up to sixty feet the moral effect on the crew would be considerable and might force the submarine to surface."[27]

Lieutenant Hersing of U-21 German submarine commander's depth-charge remembrance, "...when depth-charged after firing two torpedoes at a convoy off the south-west coast of Ireland. He was forty meters under water, and every ten seconds charges detonated at depths of ten, twenty-five, and fifty meters in all directions...for five hours the Germans in their steel hull could hear the explosions...all round them, and the hollow roaring sound of the destroyers' propellers overhead."[28] The moral and psychological impact on the crew could be significant.

Long-term Depth Charge Problem

Success with the depth charge hinges on the length of time between awareness of the enemy submarine and the arrival of the weapon in the proximity of the target, as the depth charge is a proximity weapon, not contact. This time is sometimes referred to as blind time. With the early depth charges and their sink rate of the order of 6 feet per second a target at 150 feet requires 26 seconds after launch for the depth charge to be at the point of explosion. With submarines having underwater speeds of the order of 10 knots, one minute provides about 100 feet of travel. This factor plus other response times by the pursuing vessel did not make for success. Submarine operating depths and speed on the surface and below increased throughout the 20th century. Deeper submarine operations also lessened the depth charge's effectiveness. Increased sea pressure reduces explosive force. The time required for a surfaced submarine to submerge decreased. Early underwater sound detection devices lost contact with the enemy submarine when close and required increased speed by the targeting vessel to minimize blind time. Some early detection systems required the ASW vessel to be dead in the water. Charges could be in the water after the contact was lost. Mired in these changes, depth charge design and tactics demanded serious attention.

Depth Charge at Sea

Early use of the depth charge did not always insure success as in the case of an action in July 1916 when the patrol craft HMS *Salmon* attacked the UC-7 with depth charges and the UC-7 escaped. It became clear that large numbers of depth charges were required to raise the probability of damage to a U-boat to better than luck. During World War I, both sides were limited in their antisubmarine efforts by the lack of depth charges in adequate numbers.

The 1915 successful intrusion into the Sea of Marmora via the Dardanelles by a number of British submarines was not marred by the use of depth charges. It is interesting that the Turkish Navy then under the guidance of Germany did [29] not use depth charges that were introduced by Germany early in 1915

However, by 1916 the depth charge was in broad use by Germany, Great Britain with France and Italy introducing the weapon at about the same time. The British submarines operating in the Baltic Sea in the fall of 1917 had to think carefully about German depth charges when challenging German convoys. Throughout World War I, Germany used the float and lanyard triggering type depth charge designated C15. Failure to explode was about 50% of the time. With a 110-pound charge, a thirty-five-foot destructive radius was expected.[30]

First depth charge sinking occurred March 22, 1916. TheU-68 attacked *HMS Farnborough* a "Q-ship" off the southwest coast of Ireland.[31] The submarine's torpedo missed the surface ship which retaliated with deck gunfire and depth charges sinking the submarine with all hands.

The German submarine UB-26 was sunk near Le Havre from a depth charge fired from the French destroyer *Trombe* on April 5, 1916. The same month unsuccessful depth charge attacks on two U-boats operating in the British Isles alerted Germany to the introduction of the new weapon.

Two U-boat losses by depth charge occurred later on December 4, 1916 UC-19 in the Dover Straits and on December 6 UB-29 in the English Channel, by *HMS* destroyers *Llewellyn* and *Ariel* on December 13, 1916 two depth charges from *HMS Landrail* operating in the Straits of Dover sank the UB-29.

On 8 February 1917, destroyer *HMS Thrasher* operating off Flamborough Head, at 53.56 N 00.05 E observed the minelayer UC-39 sinking a ship. As the submarine dived, a depth charge from the destroyer burst in the UC-39's conning tower, flooding it and the control room. Forced to the surface, the submarine was sunk by the destroyer's gunfire.[32] In 1918, seventeen of the U-boat depth charge sinkings occurred around the British Coast.

According to Messimer,[33] in October 1916, the Austrian U-16 sank the Allies Italian destroyer *Nembo*. As the depth of the sinking destroyer increased, its depth charges exploded and sank the U-16. Both the Italians and the Japanese operating in the Mediterranean in the later years of war made effective use of depth charges in defeating U-boats.

Although in short supply by 1915, Allied ships began using depth charges. These waterproof bombs exploded at a chosen depth. At first, these were not very effective and between 1915 and the end of 1917, depth charges accounted for only nine U-boats. By 1918, they were improved. With more depth charges available, twenty-two U-boats were destroyed. Improvement included a hydrostatic trigger with a dial for depth providing settings between 50 and 200 feet. Orders for improved depth charges were 10,000 in July 1917, with 20,000 ordered January 1918.[35] It has been estimated that as many as 1,745 per month were expended during the later part of 1918.[36] The total number of depth charges expended during WWI has been estimated at 16,500. Significantly higher numbers have been reported.

WWI Monthly Depth Charge Use [34]

Year	Number
1916	100
1917	200
1918	500

United States and the depth charge WW I

Frequently details about submarines and associated systems are under the heading of secret. Depth charges were no exception. Countries using depth charges placed the construction and methods of exploding them in the secret realm. It follows that United States, a neutral nation, was not fully aware of depth charge developments and progress until the declaration of war in April 1917. Prior to that time, some initiatives were taken.

Before United States entered the War and recognizing the need for the new weapon, the United States Bureau of Ordnance (February 1917) selected a depth charge design with 50 pounds of explosive that used the float and line trigger mechanism and a depth capability of 25 to 100 feet. Designated as MK I, an order for 10,000 was placed and they were available upon entry into the War in April 1917 at a time when the U-boats chose unrestricted warfare. With the MK1, a speed of 5 knots or greater was specified for the depth charging vessel.

The limitations of the float and line trigger mechanism brought attention to the British hydrostatic technique that replaced that method. The United States Navy was not comfortable with the British designed depth charge hydrostatic trigger. Their method was found to detonate prematurely in the water and the exposed external firing device that protruded several inches beyond the head of the cylindrical depth charge container could fire while handling. Detonation during transportation was another consideration.

Critical of the safety and effectiveness of the British hydrostatic depth charge trigger, a careful examination of the British depth was undertaken. With safety and reliability a priority, the Bureau of Ordnance tested different ways to detonate. "Various means of effecting this explosion were tested, including slow-burning time trains, buoys paying out wire, and hydrostatic pressure devices."[37] This effort led to a new development.

Chester T. Minkler

One of the investigators working at the Naval Torpedo Station in Newport, Rhode Island, developed a new device to detonate the charges. The investigator was Chester T. Minkler, a young and experienced Bureau of Ordnance engineer of mines and explosives at the Naval Torpedo Station. He devised a new hydrostatic trigger that corrected the shortcomings. The new device also allowed greater depth settings and included an external control for setting the desired depth for explosion.[38] Minkler received his patent in August 1917 and turned it over to the United States Government. It should be noted that in October 1929 the British unsuccessfully challenged Minkler's patent rights.

When the United States entered the war, an exchange of information with the British made it clear that 50 pounds of explosive was not effective. The 300 pound charge being used by the British was adopted. New and stronger submarines mandated a larger charge. In 1940, the U. S. Navy ran depth charge tests against an operational submarine (for most of the test, moored underwater without crew), and determined that 300 pounds of TNT was not very effective; the explosive charge was doubled to 600 pounds.

The American version of the Newport designed depth charge with the newly patented detonator was designated Mark II. An initial contract was placed in July 1917 for the manufacture of 10,000 with first deliveries in the fall of that year. The British government adopted the MKII in 1918 and placed a request to the Bureau of Ordnance to contract 15,000 depth charges[39] With some modifications, an additional U.S. Navy order for 20,000 Mark II depth charges was placed in the spring of 1918. The United States during World War I let contracts for a total of 72,000 depth charges. With the end of the war, unfulfilled contracts were closed where feasible.

A submarine chaser dropping MKI charges with 50 pounds of explosive specified at least a 25-foot depth setting and ship's speed of 7 knots. The MKII with the 300 pounds of explosive making a total weight of 420 pounds and a dropping rate of 6 feet per second had a 50-foot depth limitation for detonation and a required speed of 15 knots. A 200-foot maximum depth was another parameter.

An order for 20,000 MKIII with a 300-foot depth setting capability was placed in July 1917. At about the same time,1000 MK IV with a 600 pound charge and a weight of 745 pounds were ordered and available overseas in September 1918.[40]

New Convoying Initiatives

By May 8, 1917 (about a month after United States entered World War I), the first six of 36 US destroyers arrived and were ported at Queenstown in southern Ireland for duty. At the same time as the arrival of the destroyers, the Allies began a significant push to convoy merchant ships with naval escorts as a means of countering the U-boats. Successful convoying required a multitude of escort ships, and the destroyers were available to escort convoys and to aid merchant ships shelled or damaged by U-boats.

U-58

The first German submarine sunk by the U.S. Navy in World War I was the U-58. Commissioned in 1916, U-58 was 219.8 feet long with a submerged speed of 8 knots and 14 on the surface and a maximum operating depth of 164 feet. It was the first U-boat kill of the war by American destroyers. On November 17, 1917, as the *USS Fanning* (DD 37) patrolled in the eastern Atlantic in the company of other destroyers, Fanning's lookouts sighted a periscope.

Fanning attacked and the first depth charge pattern scored a hit. The *Nicholson* (DD 52 accompanying the *Fanning* made a depth charge pass. The U-58 broke the surface. It has been inferred that the explosions jammed the submarine's diving gear and the U-boat plunged towards the bottom and that at about 300 feet, the submarine blew ballast and shot toward the surface. When the U-boat broke the surface the destroyers shelled. The submarine crew came out on deck with hands raised in surrender. The *Fanning* maneuvered to pick up survivors as the submarine sunk. Forty survivors were taken prisoner. Two different locations are mentioned regarding the location of the engagement. One site is near the Hebrides, the other some distance away from the Hebrides off Milford Haven, Wales at 5132N 0521W.[41] in the Bristol Channel. This was the first of two U-boats sunk by US Navy destroyers in World War I.[42]

World War I Ends

By mid-1918 and during the closing months of the War, improving success of merchant ship convoying and the enhanced performance of depth charges on the destroyers with stern racks, K-guns, and Y-guns, the life expectancy of a U-boat was six combat patrols. Further, U-boat attacks were beginning to be limited to nighttime.

October 21, 1918 three weeks before the Armistice, the British ex-cargo vessel *Privet* operating as a "Q" ship encountered the U-34 in the Straits of Gibraltar the attempting to leave the Mediterranean. *Privet's* depth charges and gunfire sinking the submarine made the U-34 the last U-boat casualty of the War.

The U-34 was observed leaving a trail of light in the water as it was exiting the Mediterranean. *Privet* tracked down and destroyed the submarine. Later it was suggested that a possible source of the aforementioned light was the bioluminescent glow resulting from the disturbance of the plankton by the motion of the submarine.

Even closer to the Armistice on November 10, 1918, (the eve of the Armistice), that minelayer *HMS Ascot* was torpedoed on the northeast coast of England. The central role of the U-boats during the entire five years of World War I persisted until the end.

A mid-1960s appraisal of the depth charge as the War closed is appropriate. "The weapon with the greatest future was the depth charge independent of geography wherever and whenever U-boats made attack on shipping."[43]

World War II Comment

"At the start of the Second World War the stern-released depth charge was the only viable A/S weapon"[44]

Entering World War II, the available depth charge capability heavily reflected the status at the end of World War I. Five years of the new World War saw significant changes in the depth charges and their tactical use. Early depth charges were still primarily rolled over the stern of antisubmarine craft or flung out to the side of the pursuing craft using the K-gun or the Y-gun.

Features of the wartime depth charge developments included the ability to fire ahead of the vessel pursuing the submarine and deliver a wide semicircular pattern of charges. This capability, associated with much-improved underwater detection reduced the blind time between enemy submarine detection and weapon delivery. In some instances, wartime systems were implemented that coordinated depth charge firing with the sonar system's enemy submarine detection.

During the entire World War II, the generic depth charge, ("ashcan"), underwent improvement and refinement. In a timely fashion, United States and Great Britain through research and speedy development produced various new antisubmarine warfare weapon systems of the firing ahead type augmenting the basic depth charge. At the same time, improving sonar systems enhanced the effectiveness of depth charges systems with their ability to locate and track the enemy submarines. The significant changes came in the firing ahead capability.

Reviewing U-boat losses for the period August 1942 to May 1943 cited by Tarrant demonstrates the extensive use and effectiveness of the depth charge.

During that 10-month period, 150 U-boats were sunk with 127 or about 85% of the sinking a result of depth charging.[45]

Endnotes

[25] Jellicoe, *op., cit.,* p. 61.
[26] G. A. Stackhouse Jr., *The Anglo-American Atlantic Convoy System in World War I, 1917-18.* (Volumes I and II), University of Michigan, Ann Arbor, MI, 1983, p. 350.
[27] Jellicoe, *op. cit.,* p. 61.
[28] Dorling, *op. cit.,* p. 268.
[29] Sims, op, cit., p. 94
[30] Messimer, *op. cit.,* p. 221
[31] Gilbert, *op. cit.,* p236
[32] Dorling , *op. cit.,* p. 269
[33] Messimer, *op. cit.,* p. 206.
[34] www.ku.edu/-kansite/ww_one/naval/br 1669.htm, p. 2.
[35] Jellicoe, op. cit., p 81
[36] Tarrant, *op, cit.,* p. 42.
[37] US *Navy Ordnance Activities, op. cit.,* p. 98.
[38] US *Navy Ordnance Activities, op. cit.,* p. 99.
[39] Evelyn M. Cherpak, "Chester t. Minkler and The Development of Naval Underwater Ordnance", Newport History: *Bulletin of the Newport Historical Society,* Vol. 59, Part 4.
[40] US *Navy Ordnance Activities, op. cit.,* p. 101.
[41] http://uboat.net/wwi/boats/index.html?boat=58
[42] *Dictionary of American Naval Fighting Ships,* Navy Historical Society, 1981.
[43] Grant, *op. cit.,* p. 169.
[44] Willem Hackman, *Seek and Strike,* Her Majesty's Stationery Office, London, 1964, p. 303.
[45] Tarrant, *op. cit.,* p. 117-119.

Matthew Fontaine Maury:

Naval Officer, Scientist, and Oceanographer

Introduction

In a millennial hall of maritime fame, we could probably find a great candidate for each century. The particular defining contribution may not be as earthshaking as the impact on maritime navigation of our contemporary high technology Global Positioning Satellite (GPS). But in his own time and place, the contribution by the candidate could have been as significant. For example, the creativity, patience and genius of 18th century John Harrison with his chronometer and Salem's own Nathaniel Bowditch quickly and easily come to mind. Matthew Fontaine Maury, a candidate for the 19th century, sometimes seems to be lost from the pantheon of maritime fame.

In retrospect, Maury was always interested in large problems and questions frequently of worldwide interest. It is his development and introduction of reliable and useful charts of the seas beginning in 1847 that take highest place. One hundred and fifty years ago, Maury understood the need for and the value of charts of the sea made from complete and up to date oceanographic findings.

Maury succeeded in spite of the attitudes of some of his peers, superiors, and others regarding his interest in scientific matters and methods that were considered unusual for a naval officer at that time. He spent nearly twenty years in Washington, where even with his consistent integrity and desire to achieve in ways to help others, the always rampant political scuffling hounded him and later followed him south to the Confederacy in 1861 with a cost. Optimizing the use of limited resources with a tendency toward the practical are other Maury trademarks. Further characteristics include his creative ability in a variety of scientific areas, which continued productively throughout his entire life. The extensive Maury holdings at the National Archives attest to his legacy.[*]

Mid-1855

If Lieutenant Matthew Fontaine Maury USN, the sitting superintendent of the Depot of Charts and Instruments, found time in his busy mostly fifteen-hour days, he could look back with perhaps more than modest pride on his thirty years of Navy service and his family life. The next decades would demand as much from Maury as the preceding ones.

His work at the Depot starting in 1842 and national and international acknowledgment of his achievements as superintendent by the 1850s were a matter of record. In his position, he came to know nine Presidents. The fact that he was 19 years in the grade of Lieutenant while promotion remained elusive probably caused some consternation. International honors he had, but at the moment, the continuing bickering with Joseph Henry at the Smithsonian Institute and Alexander Bache at the Coast Survey must have been annoying to him. The underlying source of the friction seems to have arisen from Maury's great practical successes on a grand scale and his perception by the general public and others as a man of science. His self-education and lack of academic credentials seems to have made a difference to some in the Washington scene.

Looking Back

In 1855 and 49 years old, Maury's life divided into several stages, connected but distinct. First there was his early life with his family on a rural cotton farm in a remote

---

[*] Lewis J. Darter Jr., "Federal Archives Relating to Matthew Fontaine Maury." American Neptune, Vol. 1: p. 149-158.

part of Tennessee until he was 19. Next, the initial phase of his Navy career as a midshipman and passed midshipman included almost nine years of consecutive sea duty on three cruises mostly in the South Pacific. By the end of his second cruise from September 1826-June 1830, Maury was on the sloop-of-war *Vincennes* when it made the first circumnavigation of the globe by an American warship, the second to go to China. By June 1831, Maury was making his second trip around Cape Horn, this time as acting sailing master on the sloop-of-war *Falmouth* bound for squadron duty off the West Coast of South America.

His duties on the *Falmouth* included directing the officer of the watch on the vessel's course and how much sail to carry. He would also be the captain's navigator. In preparation, Maury looked for information on the winds and currents to be expected in rounding the Horn. His searches in New York and elsewhere were unsuccessful. He consulted libraries, merchant ships, and ship chandlers but failed. Lack of accurate information on winds and currents shaped his planning for the forthcoming voyage and did not go unnoticed.

During the following three years off the West Coast of South America, he served as first lieutenant on several Navy ships in the squadron and returned on the frigate *Boston.* Upon returning, probably highlighted in his memory was his marriage in 1834 to his Virginia cousin Ann Herndon from nearby Fredericksburg, Virginia, and the following year the birth of the first of his eight children.

At that time, the Navy had a very limited number of vessels with one ship of the line, three frigates, and some small ships. The number of officers' billets was small. This could mean years on the beach at half pay for officers waiting a ship assignment. Maury was ashore for the next several years, with the exception of a short tour aboard a

Navy ship doing hydrographic work along the East Coast of the United States.

In 1839, while visiting his parents in Tennessee whom he had not seen in nine years, he received orders for sea duty aboard the brig *Consort*, then at the New York Navy Yard. In October, returning north for duty by mail stagecoach, the coach overturned. Maury's right leg was severely damaged by a thighbone fracture badly set, and for the rest of his life he walked with a limp. Slowly recovering in Ohio, he missed his ship in New York but by January1840 was at his home in Fredericksburg. From then on, his fitness for sea duty would always be in contention and occasionally questioned. Convalescence was slow, and during these years his writing skills emerged further.

Two years after recovering from the accident, 1841 brought hope for a possible return to sea duty in the Pacific Squadron aboard the frigate *United States*. Then, as a result of efforts by his friends, relatives and several of Fredericksburg's medical doctors, a letter was sent, unknown to Maury, to the Secretary of the Navy advising him that Maury because of his leg injury was in no physical condition for sea duty aboard a man-of-war. In November, surprised and possibly embarrassed by the letter, he asked the Secretary to be relieved from orders to sea. His request was approved.

Superintendent of the Navy's Depot of Charts and Instruments

After three years of inactive duty, Maury reported July 4, 1842 as superintendent of the Navy's Depot of Charts and Instruments in Washington. Established in 1830, the Depot was the first scientific institution in the Navy. It was the center for all Navy nautical and astronomical research.

What did he bring to his Depot assignment? His nine years at sea in all the oceans certainly provided a good credential. Between 1838 and 1841 while ashore, he wrote widely on civilian and Navy matters and built up a favorable public readership. Prominent among his topics were the need for a Naval Academy, the use of steamships, and recommendations for the Navy to establish Bureaus in lieu of a Board of Commissioners. His pen names included Will Watch, Union Jack, Ben Bow and Harry Bluff. The public interest created by the articles made it necessary to reveal Maury as Harry Bluff in July 1841. For his views, comments, and recommendations, Maury was not only popular, but also highly regarded and very well known. His popularity led to his being considered for the position of Secretary of the Navy. Maury was not interested.

His publications on navigation and oceanography prior to his superintendence included "On the Navigation of Cape Horn" and "Plan of an Instrument for Finding the True Lunar Distance", published in July 1834. These were followed in 1836 by a navigation book, A New Theoretical and Practical Treatise on Navigation. The motivation for writing the book stemmed from his desire to provide a text appropriate for the novice navigator and midshipmen, not the veteran mariner. He felt the existing texts were aimed at those whose sea experience was extensive.

This was the first scientific book written and published by an American naval officer. In the *Southern Literary Messenger*, a Richmond, Virginia publication frequently dealing with Army and Navy topics, the assistant editor and critical reviewer Edgar Allan Poe lauded the book.

The book was a success. Professors, naval officers, and Nathaniel Bowditch commended it. It took the place of Bowditch's Practical Navigator as a textbook for junior Navy officers and in 1837 was placed on every ship in the Navy. Later in 1845, when the U. S. Naval Academy was established, it became one of the standard texts used. From the textbook and his other writings for Navy reform, Maury was well known when he arrived at the Depot. He brought his seamanship, experience, his published book and papers, and a totally inquiring nature. A few months after the initial introduction of the navigation book in 1836, Maury, the Passed Midshipman and author, became a Lieutenant in the U. S. Navy.

Almost immediately after assuming the superintendent's work, Maury became involved in developing improved charts of the sea. However, there were additional assignments. The Depot's work included building the new Navy astronomical observatory, equipping, staffing and placing it in operation. Between 1845 and 1855, under Maury's leadership the Observatory catalogued 100,000 stars and became known as one of the nation's important scientific institutes.

Maritime Scene Mid-19th Century

With sails still the predominant propulsion mode, wind and current charts were significant. By the middle of the century, merchant shipping and the number of ships around the world continued to grow. In competition with the sailing vessel, the steamship was a strong and growing presence in the 1840s and 50s also not in the large numbers that would prevail by the end of the Century. An examination of the front page of the New York Shipping and Commerce List reporting ship arrivals and clearings for January 22, 1851 shows the numbers of steamers and steamships to be very small compared to hundreds of barques, brigs, and schooners listed for that day.

Sails for propulsion, especially on the longer voyages, ruled for another quarter century. The Navy itself only gradually warmed to the notion of using steam for warships, and by then it was past mid-century. A coal burning Navy vessel was difficult to accept by some. With sails dominating, the winds and currents still were among the main challenges to shipmasters.

Increased shipping came in part from the discovery and exploitation of gold in California. The sea paths from the East Coast to California around Cape Horn or to the Isthmus of Panama with a trek to the Pacific Ocean side and up to San Francisco by sail were long. From England merchant ships sailing to Australia and return took significant amounts of sailing time with the limited information and understanding about seaways available before Maury's wind and current charts. Further, steamers at that time frequently were equipped with sails either in an auxiliary or predominant propulsion role and winds and currents still counted. The 150 clipper ships at their peak validated Maury's wind and current charts.

Wind and Current Charts

Assuming office at the Depot, Maury remembered his experience in 1831 when as a sailing master preparing for his second trip around the Horn at the tip of South America he was unable to locate adequate wind and current charts. Not long after arriving at the Depot, Maury took action to increase understanding and knowledge of wind and currents, which he knew was lacking.

"Less than two months after he took up his post he had to admit that the files of the office could furnish no hydrographical information as to certain portions of the Gulf of Mexico. Charts of naval vessels were found to be over one hundred years old and quite useless. In 1845 he wrote the Secretary that the office did not know whether there was a frigate harbor on the east side of Florida, a remarkable circumstance since we have owned Florida for more than a quarter of century since and since we purchased it chiefly for national defense."*

Maury started his research for developing better charts by making use of what was available. The Depot was the archive for Navy ship logs and official Navy records, not in the sense of an organized collection but as a place for storage. Initially, old ship logs were examined to determine the nature of winds and currents on the Atlantic. Because many of the available logs covered the north-south path to and from Rio de Janeiro, these were the first analyzed. This effort required scrutinizing thousands of pages to find data on wind, rain, current, fog, and other navigational information in the logs. From these efforts, charts were made showing the best sailing paths for the seasons of the year.

As Maury worked with old logs, their inadequacies were realized. He came up with the idea for a new type of abstract log sheets for mariners to use to provide data that would lead to making useful wind and current information for future navigators. He requested and received approval from Commodore William M. Crane, head of the newly established Bureau of Ordnance and Hydrography, to implement the log sheets and have the data sent to the Depot. The Bureau system implemented at this time replaced the old Board of Commissioners and provided the basis for Navy management until the last half of the 20th century. Prior to Congressional action mandating the Bureau system, Maury was one of the voices favorable to its establishment.

In the fall of 1842, a Bureau circular to captains and masters of merchant vessels requested that they send navigational, meteorological and hydrographic data observed

---

*Louis J. Darter Jr., "Federal Archives Relating to Matthew Fontaine Maury." American Neptune, Vol. 1: p. 154

by the ships to the Depot. Maury needed information on currents, depths, salinity, temperatures of the oceans, and of wind patterns from direct observation to develop his charts.

Navy captains were slow to respond to the request to fill in and forward the blank charts provided. However, the response overall provided enough data so that the following March Maury published "Directions for approaching the West Coast of Sumatra" based on the newly collected information.

By 1851, 1000 sets of abstract logs were sent to Washington. The number grew and by the latter part of the century 1887, 26 million filled-in charts had been provided from all sources.

The first wind and current charts for ships in the open seas were published in 1847. During the first year of publication, 5000 copies of the charts were made available. Charts saved time and dollars in long sea voyages. The trip from New York to Rio de Janeiro was reduced from 55 to between 35 and 40 days.

Sailing tracks for the North Atlantic came out in 1847. As charts covering the South Atlantic and the Pacific became available in 1849, sailing times steadily lowered. An 1850s estimate indicated $15 million savings per year from the use of charts. The round trip from Great Britain to Australia and New Zealand dropped from 240 to 160 days. In 1852, the passage from New York to San Francisco decreased to 92 days from 118. With as many as 145 clipper ships using charts and saving time and money on their extended voyages, Maury's celebrity status grew. Savings in Indian Ocean crossings were estimated at $1million. Overall, British commerce saved $10 million per year and United States more than $2 million per year.

In a celebrated New York-to-California race in the fall of 1852 between four clipper ships, Maury's <u>Wind and Current Charts</u> played a significant role for all the contestants. Maury criticized Captain Nickels of *Flying Fish*, the winner. "So forgetting that the charts are founded on the experience of great numbers who had gone before him, Nickels, being tempted turned a deaf ear to the caution, and flung away three whole days and more of most precious time, dallying in the doldrums."*

After this, captains used the charts and sailing directions and filled in the Abstract Logs and sent them to the Observatory. "By the end of 1851, Maury could report a thousand American ships on the high seas were faithfully recording this information and at the end of each voyage sending it in to him."**

In the decade before the Civil War, Maury became one of the most famous men in the world. These years were marked by success after success always in some practical scientific area. However, adversity did strike at mid-decade.

International Science

In part due to his instigation and in conjunction with British scientists, Maury helped to foster the first International Conference on Meteorology held at Brussels August 23, 1853. The goal of the conference was to create an environment of cooperation between the attending nations leading to a universal system for observations at sea. Initially Maury would have preferred the conference to cover both land and sea.

----

*Frances Lee Williams, Matthew Fontaine Maury: Scientist of the Sea, Rutgers University Press, 1963, p. 191.
** Ibid. p. 192.

Belgium, Denmark, France, Great Britain, Netherlands, Norway, Portugal, Russia, Sweden and the United States accepted invitations. The meetings continued until 8 September and concluded with the acceptance of an international standard for abstract logs, one for men-of-war and one for merchant shipping, and the establishment of the International Hydrographic Bureau.

Maury attended as the United States representative and was well received. Through these meetings he came to know and develop close relationships with important international European scientists. In particular, he came to know Baron Von Humboldt, a major figure in physical geography.

Other Mid-1850s achievements

Transatlantic Telegraph Cable

Charged with the laying of a transatlantic telegraph cable, Cyrus W. Field began discussions with Maury in 1853 regarding best placement of the cable. Maury's knowledge of the ocean bottom and depth derived from several years of measurements made earlier at the behest of Maury and with help from Congress. In 1854, Maury published the first bathymetric chart of the Atlantic Ocean from 10° S to 50° N and provided guidance to Field. The depths identified were to 24,000 feet. Later, when the project was successfully completed, Field is reported as saying, "Maury furnished the brain...England gave the money...I did the work." This brought more praise and fame to Maury.

North Atlantic Steamer Lanes

In the 1850s, as steamer traffic across the Atlantic increased, ship collisions and loss of life caused great concern. A particular tragedy on September 20, 1854 on the

Grand Banks 50 miles east of Cape Race, Newfoundland called the public's attention to collisions at sea on the paths between United States and Europe. The French ship Vesta, with watertight compartments and iron construction, struck the Arctic, a side-wheeler passenger liner en route from Liverpool to New York.* The Arctic sank in four hours; 350 people died; and the 87 survivors were all men. The sinking was a highly publicized event and brought about attention to the increased density of steamers in transit at one time on the high seas.

Maury was asked concerning the practicability of laying down separate lanes for ships plying between Europe and America. He conceived a plan for two lanes, one to go and one to return on appropriate great circle paths with room to maneuver. The plan, "Chart showing two steamer lanes each twenty miles wide, North Atlantic," was published in 1855. The U.S. Navy encouraged the use of the plan. Some steamship lines put it to use, but it was near the end of the century before it was fully subscribed. Like a great deal of Maury's work, the end results provided practical solutions to difficult problems.

During the next seven years, his recognition at home and abroad saw him made a member of 45 learned societies, 20 of which were in foreign countries. Denmark, France, Portugal, Russia, Norway, Sweden, Holland, and Austria found it appropriate to recognize and reward Maury. In 1860, the Pope, whose papal fleet was involved in the data collection and benefited from Maury's wind and current charts, sent him a set of thirteen medals in appreciation.

----

*Comdr. A. G. Brown (retired), "The Arctic Disaster: Maury's Motivation, "United States Naval Institute Proceedings" 94:1 (January 1968), pp. 78-83

Physical Geography of the Sea

The sweep of Maury's interests is probably best reflected in his book <u>Physical Geography of the Sea</u>. As a personal enterprise, he wrote at home after working hours, completing and publishing it in a little more than a year. The book had five printings in the first year 1855. This first modern oceanographic textbook remained continuously in print for 25 years in the United States and England and was printed in six continental languages. Like most things having the Maury stamp, the book was large, almost 500 pages. With the book the science of oceanography was opened. There were many early critics, but a 1930 comment called the theoretical treatment remarkable considering the time when Maury wrote it.

This friendly comment aside, some of Maury's contemporaries and other scientists later in the century were not always in agreement with some of his explanations and hypothetical generalizations of the sea. That he contributed to science and navigation is not challenged. It was Maury's interpretations and speculations in the Geography that were brought to task during his lifetime and after his passing. In 1963, the same year that Williams's book appeared, John Leighly of the University of California at Berkeley edited the Geography. * In a 30 page Introduction, Leighly documents many of the challenges and strongly attests to Maury's flaws in his scientific thinking. Leighly does not entirely excoriate Maury. He does allow that the book did exert some limited scientific influence. Frances Leigh Williams in her 1963 precise biography observes.

----

*John Leighly (editor), <u>The Physical Geography of the Sea and Its Meteorology: by Matthew Fontaine Maury,</u> The Belknap Press of Harvard University Press, Cambridge, Massachusetts, 1963, Introduction.

"But Maury was a pioneer investigator of the phenomenon of the seas; and although research in later years proves some of his concepts wrong, he was a bold workman who believed beginnings had to be made."*

The introduction to the first edition in 1855 clarifies his rationale for wind and current data and how the new book came to be. He wrote "The primary object of the Wind and Current Charts out of which has grown this Treatise on the Physical Geography of the Sea was to collect the experience of every navigator as to the winds and currents of the ocean, to discuss his observations upon them, and to present the world with the results on charts for the improvement of commerce and navigation."

Adversity

In 1855, when Maury was a highly recognized international scientific figure, Congress passed the Navy reform bill, which Maury favored. His published writings under several pseudonyms encouraged reform and changes in the Navy. His recommendations included the Navy's adaptation of the Bureau system for managing the Navy and establishment of a Naval Academy, both of which came to pass.

Another of the reform measures passed by Congress created a selection board of Navy officers to review the careers and suitability of Navy officers for sea duty. The board was sometimes referred to as "the plucking board." The convening board of Navy officers held secret deliberations and kept no records. It was their

---

*Frances Leigh Williams, Matthew Fontaine Maury: Scientist of the Sea, Rutgers University Press, New Brunswick, NJ, 1963, p. 260

recommendation that Maury be placed on inactive duty. Unaware of this action Maury, with thirty years of service, was advised of this in September 1855. It took more than two and a half years of vigorous contesting involving Congress, a court of inquiry, and others for this action to be rectified. In January 1858, Maury was reinstated by President Buchanan and promoted to Commander.

During the Congressional hearings related to Maury's return, Senators Stephen R. Mallory of Florida and Jefferson Davis of Mississippi strongly opposed returning Maury to active duty. It is ironical that a few years later in April 1861, when Maury elected to return to Virginia and join the Confederate Navy, he would encounter Davis as the President of the Confederacy and Mallory as the Secretary of the Confederate Navy. Most of Maury's service to the Confederate Navy seems to have been impacted by their attitude toward him.

In April 1861, a little more than three years after his reinstatement, Maury began his career in the Confederate Navy as a scientist. During his first year with the Confederacy, he investigated and successfully demonstrated electrically detonated mines both underwater and on land. Partially due to Maury's innovative work, most of the 58 Federal ships sunk during the Civil War were lost due to mines than from all other causes combined. The uneasy relationship with Mallory and Davis probably brought him the role of Confederate Envoy in England for the last three years of the Civil War.

Without amnesty to return home from England, Maury served briefly in Mexico as an advisor on scientific and colonization activities for Emperor Maximilian. While in Mexico, he was instrumental in the successful introduction of cinchona plantations as a source for quinine. Back in England, and with President Johnson granting amnesty, Maury was able to return to U.S. during September 1867.

Several offers to lead academic institutions in the south were proffered. He chose the Virginia Military Institute and on September 10, 1868, and was appointed professor of physics. His productivity never faltered as he entered the last five years of his life. The state of Virginia honored Maury by placing his tomb between Presidents Monroe and Tyler.

Captain Miles P. DuVal, Jr., in his book <u>Matthew Fontaine Maury: Benefactor of Mankind</u> summarizes a great deal of Maury's goal: "the military role of Navy is to control the seas, to accomplish this goal the Navy must know all about them."

Sea Mines, the Submarine's Adversary and Weapon:

1775 to 1918

Part I

Sea Mines
> *Location: shallow water, rivers, harbors, Arctic,*
> *continental shelf, deep oceans*
> *Use: blockades, interdiction, barriers*
> *Purpose: offensive or defensive*
> *Delivery: aircraft, submarine, ship, barge, torpedo,*
> *rocket, hand*
> *Target: afloat or below the sea, low flying aircraft*[1]

The Beginning

Stating with precision the beginning of a technology and identifying the exact time, place and inventor or discoverer is a challenge. The Greeks are credited with developing the first sea mine in the seventh century BC. Sulfur, naphtha, and nitre in a barrel were set afire and placed so as to have the tide or current move the barrel to an enemy vessel and set it on fire. They learned that the weapon, with the aid of a catapult, could be land-based or ship-based.[2]

With the sea mine (sometimes called submarine mine), Dutch roots are found in the 16th century "…when the Dutch loaded vessels with large amounts of explosives and sent these drifting mines against an enemy ship or an enemy's shore fortification." In 1585, Federico Gianibelli, an Italian working for the Dutch against Spain, sent two "bomb ships" to drift into a bridge over the River Scheldt at Antwerp, Belgium. The bomb ships exploded against the bridge, tearing a 200-foot gap in it. This was the first time a large explosive charge was used in naval warfare.[3] China is credited with using explosive powder for signaling and fireworks in the 10th century. It has been noted that the English may have used the first naval mines in 1627 at the siege of La Rochelle when they launched "floating petards" unsuccessfully against the French navy. Sea mines evolved through the years from the contributions of many professionals and some amateurs.

In the centuries following the Dutch efforts, gradual acceptance, evolution, and growth of the mine as an underwater weapon took place. An accounting of mine usage at the end of the World War II determined that the Axis and Allied forces laid 500,000 submarine mines. This unique weapon with offensive and defensive capability also does not differentiate between friend and foe. Further, sowing mines and minesweeping are both considerable challenges. The results obtained with sea mines in World War I and World War II established the mine as a formidable offensive and defensive weapon.

Colonial Period

In 1751, Benjamin Franklin (with his usual prescience) advised regarding how to use electricity to discharge gunpowder but it was not until the Civil War that greater use of electrical detonation applied to sea mines was invoked.

David Bushnell, builder of the one-man submersible *Turtle*, is known as the father of mine warfare. Bushnell's mines with flintlock detonators, adjusted for firing by a light shock, were oaken-staved kegs 14½ inches in height 13-inches in diameter filled with explosives.

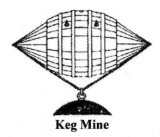

Keg Mine

In December of 1777, Bushnell set mines adrift on the Delaware River to be carried by the tide to the target enemy vessels at Philadelphia. However, erratic river currents and intervening ice floes prevented the mines from damaging the enemy vessels. During the Revolution limpet and floating contact mines used against the British ships on the Hudson and Delaware Rivers did not have great success other than deterrence. Mechanically detonated sea mines found their initial place in underwater warfare with these colonial designs. In some quarters sea mines were considered as sneak weapons and not chivalrous.

19th Century

Robert Fulton (1765-1815)

Robert Fulton, famous for his steamboats, was an artist, inventor, submarine advocate and underwater weapon innovator. During thirteen years of Fulton's nineteen-year stay (1787-1806) in England and France, the two countries were at war. He built and demonstrated sea mines and a submarine (*Nautilus)* with support at various times from both belligerents. Later, when he returned to the United States, his submarine proposal included a steam engine for propulsion.

Fulton's mine designs included contact explosion, timed explosion, using clock mechanisms to trigger the mine, and mines attached at the end of long spars in close proximity to the enemy vessel. His clockwork mechanism for mine detonation was adjustable from 4 minutes to 4 hours. Extensive experimentation and modeling were hallmarks of Fulton's inventions and their demonstration. On October 15, 1805, Fulton, funded by the Royal Navy, demonstrated a mine's effectiveness off Walmer, England. The 200-ton Danish brig *Dorothea* was totaled with the explosion of Fulton's mine.[4] The mine (2 feet long and 12 inches in diameter), filled with 180 pounds of gunpowder and a clockwork mechanism set for an explosion to occur in 18 minutes, accomplished the complete destruction of the brig. He suggested that in case of war, plantings of 100 anchored mines would be required at the selected sites.

His recommendations to the Royal Navy included blockading British ports with mines to stem potential French intrusion. Fulton also proposed mining the harbors of Plymouth, Portsmouth, Tor Bay and the Thames River. Although he did not meet with complete success in negotiations with the navies of the governments regarding submarines and the use of mines to destroy enemy ships, his ideas were prophetic.

Later, in December 1806, he returned to the United States and promoted sea mines as weapons for the United States Navy. After discussions with Secretary of State James Madison, Secretary of State and Secretary of the Navy Robert M. Smith, he received support and in 1807 successfully blew up a brig in New York Harbor with sea mines but only after several failed attempts. This was due to problems with proper weighting of the mines that caused them to turn over and spill the load of black powder or miss the target.

During the War of 1812, Fulton suggested the moored mine concept that brought the enemy ship to the explosive rather than delivering the explosive to the ship. Fulton quoted a price of $150 per mine, including the powder, to President James Madison including the powder. Practical detonation of mines electrically was severely limited at the time due to corrosion of the wires and , significantly, when should they be fired.[5]

The War saw mine-related actions both in the Chesapeake Bay and along the southern shoreline of Connecticut. Some of the mines modeled after Fulton did not succeed in blowing up British ships, but Royal Navy officers assigned to the blockade grasped the significance of mines and their use as a deterrent.

Near New London, Connecticut during the War of 1812, an unsuccessful mine attack on the blockading British man of war *Ramilles* produced a strong impact. "So great is the alarm and fear on board the *Ramilles* that Commodore Hardy has withdrawn his force from New London." [6]

On March 13, 1813, Congress passed an act to encourage the destruction of the armed vessels of war of the enemy. The act, sometimes referred to as the Torpedo Act of 1813, legalized the use of torpedoes as destructive weapons. Fulton's *Torpedo War and Submarine Explosions* that he wrote, illustrated, and published in 1810 raised awareness of the torpedo and led to the Torpedo Act.[7]

Generically the word torpedo refers to any explosive charge including the type of weapon now known as the mine. However, Robert Whitehead's self-propelled underwater weapon invented in 1864 appropriated the name torpedo. Earlier, Robert Fulton experimented with naval mines during the Napoleonic wars and called them torpedoes. In some references, this may cause confusion.

In the latter part of the 18th century and the first half of the 19th century extensive effort was directed toward the development and implementation of telegraphy. Telegraphy used wires and delivered an electrical impulse at a distance. An electrical impulse could also be sent along a wire to detonate a mine at a distance. Telegraphy required knowledge to make batteries, wire, wire insulation, and how to make wire waterproof while lying underwater below a river or in the water near a shore. Each of these items has application to mines detonated with an electrical impulse.

During the 19th century, the way was paved for the eventual development of the modern sea mine with the participation of many scientists, inventors, and entrepreneurs. Among those contributing to the related knowledge, experiments, and implementation were Russia, Great Britain, Bavaria, United States, France, Italy, and Prussia. During the century, how to take advantage underwater detonation of mines was a primary pursuit.

Mine Detonation with Electricity Pre-Civil War[8]

Year	Scientist	Application
1777	Alessandro Volta	Pistols, muskets and submarine *mines* fired electrically
1782	Tiberius Cavallo	Gunpowder fired at a great distance by electricity
1812	Pavel L'vovich Schilling	In Russia, a mine placed on the Neva River was detonated electrically from the opposite shore
1839	Col. Charles William Pasley	Electricity used successfully for submarine gun powder explosion in conjunction with marine salvage
1848	Werner von Siemens	Field of electrically controlled *mines* established in the approach to Kiel to deter Danish bombardment of that port during Schleswig-Holstein War. This was the first controlled moored minefield in history, and first installation in time of war. (He was one of the founding members of the Siemens Engineering dynasty)
1854-56	Moritz von Jacobi	Russia's newly-created blockade contact mines (also some shore-controlled detonation mines using chemical action for ignition) were successfully used in the defense of Kronstadt and Sveaborg in the Baltic and Sevastopol in the Black Sea in the Crimean War. The mines provided a major threat to the Royal Navy off Kronstadt.

Other work contributing to the evolution of the mine-related technology during the first half of the 19th century in Europe and United States included that of Bavarian Samuel Thomas Sommerring. In 1812, using wire insulated with India rubber and varnish, he telegraphed through 10,000 feet of cable.

Schilling, a pioneer in defensive mine warfare mentioned above, became aware of Sommerring's work and used insulated cables and a carbon-arc fuse in the mine's gunpowder for detonation. One of his demonstrations included the Tsar Alexander I as a witness.[9] By 1839, Russia institutionalized mine warfare by establishing a Committee on Underwater Experiments charged to determine the value of mines for harbor defense.[10]

In 1833 in the United States, Robert Hare (1781-1858) (a scientist, professor of chemistry at the University of Pennsylvania, and inventor) reported in the *Journal of the Franklin Institute* successfully using electricity to detonate gunpowder at a distance of 130 feet. In addition to using this method for rock blasting, he considered this method for exploding mines as a defense weapon for Fort Adams, then being built on the harbor in Newport, Rhode Island.

Fort Adams at Newport was one of dozens under construction and located at strategic waterways both along the coast and inland along rivers and lakes. The work on the forts was well along at this time, and there was significant vested interest in the forts and their role in defense: should exploding moored mines be considered as an assist for the forts or a replacement for them? National level interest In regard to the issue of forts versus sea mines as a means of defending against enemy sea forces seems to have been lacking.

Samuel Colt (1814-1862)

Colt is remembered primarily for his invention of the Colt revolver, the six-shot handgun, and later as a prominent successful mid-19th century New England gun manufacturer. His first United States patent for the revolver was obtained in 1832 when Colt was 18 years old. In the following years, as a result of his efforts to make sales of his revolver to the United States, he became known in Washington from his extensive lobbying for his guns with Congressional personnel. Colt with his broad interest in technical matters was associated with Samuel F. B. Morse, telegraph inventor, in the years leading up to Morse's epic telegraph demonstration on May 24, 1843. The shared interest was concerned with the burgeoning development and manufacture of insulated cable for telegraphy.

In 1829, Colt, fifteen years old and working for a dye company in Ware, Massachusetts, demonstrated the electrical firing of gunpowder underwater. On July 4th, he posted announcements that he would blow up a raft in Ware Pond. The event took place. The raft was demolished by the blast and onlookers dampened. There is no further record of Colt's interest in underwater mines until 1836. At that time, the United States severed diplomatic relations with France and President Jackson recommended strengthening the Navy and coast defense. Considering this, Colt configured an extensive moored mine system, Submarine Battery, to protect harbors and other coast locations. The system involved electrical detonation of moored mines, heating the powder to create explosions. Two visual observers directed the explosion under transiting enemy men-of-war. A full system at a given location would include 2500 mines. With the French diplomatic problem peacefully resolved, Colt's mine system did not receive attention.

Harbor defense improvement was again brought to Colt's attention in 1841 when the Maine boundary with New

Brunswick dispute with England was ongoing. This time, Colt succeeded in obtaining support. With a $6,000 advance from a $50,000 government appropriation for ordnance development and some private support, he conducted four publicly attended demonstrations of electrical detonation of the gunpowder. Each demonstration achieved its goal; and, in addition. There were vast numbers of spectators and wide press coverage.

Colt's Demonstrations

Date	Location	Target	Note
4 July 1842	New York Harbor	Gunboat *Boxer*	Broad attention to the concept
20 August 1842	Potomac River Washington, DC	Accomac Clam Boat (60 ton schooner)	President John Tyler and cabinet attended, 8,000 spectators; control 5 miles from target
18 October 1842	New York Harbor	Brig *Volta* (260 ton)	40,000 spectators
13 April 1844	East Branch Anacostia River, DC	Barque *Styx* 81 ft., (500 ton)	Control 2 miles from target, barque under sail at 5 knots/hour

The 1842 Webster-Ashburton Treaty resolved the differences with England and removed stimulus for immediate improvement of harbor defenses. Colt's demonstrations were successful, but the system did not gain favor or acceptance as a weapon. In Washington, there were technical challenges regarding Colt's basis for a patent that he solicited in 1844. Electrical detonation of mines was reasonably well known by the scientific community both in the United States and abroad. For example, in 1841 the method was used in India to remove a wreck from a river.

In his dealings with Washington, Colt maintained a level of secrecy that caused those in authority to challenge Colt and become suspicious of the system he wished to build. As the operation of a full-born system depended on observers to make the decision to explode the mines, there were challenges as to how the system would perform under conditions of fog or at night. Funding stopped and until the Civil War, development of the mine and mine countermeasures[11] in the United States were minimal. This curtailment of support for mines has been attributed to Colt's differences with those in Washington responsible for the development of the country's ongoing construction of coastal fortifications, the Third System forts.

The large number of spectators at Colt's four demonstrations and the ensuing newspaper coverage broadened the public's awareness of sea mines; but with no immediate government support, Colt's journey into moored mines concluded while his success as a gun inventor and manufacturer continued to grow nationally and internationally. In 1855, Colt had developed the world's largest armory in Hartford, Connecticut, where his manufacturing techniques with interchangeable parts, a production line to increase output, and a positive attitude towards employee welfare enhanced his fame.[12]

Commander Matthew Fontaine Maury (1806-1873)

From August 1825 until April 1861, the Virginian Matthew Fontaine Maury served as an officer of the United States Navy. During the first years of his long naval career, he spent almost nine years at sea mostly in the South Pacific. From 1841 until his resignation to join the newly-formed Confederate States of America, he was Superintendent of the Navy's Depot of Charts and Instruments in Washington (later the U.S. Hydrographic Office). There he attained national and international acclaim for his advances in oceanography and his 1855 book *Physical Geography of the Sea*. The book, a first on oceanography, was in continuous print for 25 years in the United States and England and was printed in six continental languages.

A few days after the declaration of war, Maury resigned from the U.S. Navy and went to Richmond. His initial role with the Confederacy was his appointment by Virginia's governor, John Letcher, to the Advisory Council on Naval Matters. Maury addressed the Confederacy's challenge of how to enhance harbor and coastal defense with the limited number of Confederate naval vessels available.

One direction of his thinking was to build a large number of small steam vessels with low freeboard (making a difficult target) and heavy firing power. With limited resources for construction, priority was given instead to the building of the ironclad *Merrimack*. The other direction of Maury's thinking was implementing mines for coastal and river defense. A particular focus of his mine investigation was electrical detonation that he pursued during his brief tenure in Richmond. For the South, controlled mines electrically detonated saw limited use primarily because of lack of reliable waterproof cable suitable for planting

In June, Maury, as a Commander in the Confederate Navy, became Chief of the Naval Bureau of Seacoast, River, and Harbor Defense of the South. With $50,000 allocated for experiments, he focused on developing and implementing mines that floated, drifted or were towed to contact enemy shipping. Some mines were placed on rams on the bows of small torpedo (mine) boats. On July 7, 1861, a little more than two months since Maury's resignation, he unsuccessfully led an expedition to explode torpedoes against the Federal fleet in Hampton Roads.

US Navy Admiral D. D. Porter noted the effectiveness of Confederate mining later in 1878. "...the difficulty in of capturing Charleston, Savannah, Wilmington, and Mobile, was in a measure owing to the fact that the approaches to these places were filled with various kinds of torpedoes, laid in groups something on the plans of Fulton and Colt, and fired by electricity."[13]

Of the various mines, the most significant and successful mines were those that were planted and detonated electrically with the aid of an observer. Limited availability of suitable electrical cable impeded broader implementation of this technique. For various reasons such as cost, and material shortages, the contact mine with its low cost and relative ease of manufacture and planting but with some operational limitations, became widely and effectively used by the South.

Torpedo stations were set up in Richmond, Wilmington, Charleston, Savannah, and Mobile. Maury remained with the Bureau until late June of 1862, when he was transferred to England. He did not return to the United States until 1868 and was not on hand to see the effectiveness of the sea mine investigations that he initiated.

Some Confederate Mines
Trip wire
Frame propeller trigger line
Beer-barrel torpedoes
Raft torpedoes with friction fuses
Buoyant torpedoes

After Maury left for England, the Confederate Congress in October of 1862 created a Torpedo Bureau for the Army and the Submarine Battery Service within the Navy's Office of Ordnance and Hydrography. The Submarine Battery Service mines accounted for sinking at least 40 Union ships. At the battle of Mobile Bay (4 August), 1864, a field of 80 mines, the first to be equipped with safety devices, was laid to defend the city. During the battle a mine destroyed the monitor *USS Tecumseh,* the newest and most powerful of all the Federal ironclads. The *Tecumseh,* constructed at a cost of about one million dollars, was destroyed by a mine with a cost of less than one hundred dollars. Later on December 9, mines detonated from shore destroyed seven of 12 Federal vessels moving up to the Roanoke River to capture Fort Branc, North Carolina.[14]

Maury was correct with his vision of mines as effective defensive weapons. During the War more Union ships were lost to mines than to any other weapon. Further, mines prior to the Civil War sometimes floated toward enemy shipping and provided opportunity for an avoidance maneuver. Mines now successfully being placed beneath the surface added a new dimension to their lethality and the consequent deterrent impact on coastal or river intruders. Neither of he navies overlooked offensive use of the mine. Both sides investigated drifting mines and the spar torpedo from torpedo boats and ironclads.

Similar to the case of other weapons, mine countermeasures slowly evolved. T. M. Melia in <u>Damn the Torpedoes: A Short History of U. S. Naval Mine</u>

Countermeasures, 1777-1991 points out that earliest countermeasures included bow watches or personnel in small boats looking for mines. Contact mines, if located were sunk with a properly placed bullet hole. Later, other countermeasures developed.

With the Confederate Navy planting the mines, the Federal forces took the initiative to counter the mines. The 1997 book *Shades of Blue and Gray* points out that the Union Navy devised a defensive mechanism, the world's first "mine sweepers." To assist Union ships transiting inland waterways of the South, first use of such a device occurred on 30 April 1862. The first countermeasure was attached to the bow of a monitor modified for minesweeping. A primary sweeping device consisted of a huge rake 65 feet long. Affixed to it were large numbers of grappling hooks, pushed ahead of a lead vessel. A symposium held in 2000 at the Navy Postgraduate School also referred to the device; "One invention was the wood and bamboo 'cow catcher'. It was designed to stand out from the Clad's bow 20 to 30 feet and acted as false front. One was attached to the monitor *USS Saugus* and used during the James River Operation. They called this device a 'torpedo catcher' or 'torpedo rake'. At the same time, the US Navy also experimented with fish nets extending from all sides of the ship to protect against contact mines." During the Civil War, of forty-three Federal ships struck by Confederate mines, twenty-seven sunk. The Confederacy's success with mines brought global attention to the mine as an effective weapon.

Post Civil War-1900

The first half of the 19th century brought improvements in mine performance and its utilization. Several European conflicts provided opportunities for implementation. This helped to establish the mine's creditability always as a deterrent even in cases where its performance was limited. Stealth quality of the mine when buried beneath the sea was recognized, an "invisible" weapon. This particular aspect of the mine brought contempt in some circles and a somewhat negative approach to its development and ultimate use. This opinion of mines persisted. Mines were judged as *"unworthy and improper to the conduct of wars"*.

Mines saw use in the Paraguayan War (1865-7-). Argentina, Brazil, and Uruguay War opposed Paraguay. Mines laid in the Paraguay River cost Brazil one monitor. Paraguay lost the war but interest in mine warfare was sustained in the Latin American navies.

European navies also began to regularly use mines detonated mechanically and electro-mechanically. For instance, during the Franco-Prussian War (1870)[15] with Franco-Prussian War 1870, the Prussians publicized the fact that they were laying mines in an attempt to keep the superior French fleet away from its ports. Realizing that merely the fear of mines might keep the French Navy at bay, the Prussians even laid dummy weapons when production of real mines ran behind schedule.

Hertz horn-50 year detonator

Developed in 1868 by the North German Defense Committee, the Hertz horn electrical detonator continued in use through the first quarter of the 20th Century. As it projected outward from the outer surface of the mine, the word horn was an apt description of its appearance. To insure contact by the passing warship (vessel) several horns were mounted. The invention is attributed variously to a person by the name of Herz or Hertz. It was adapted by Russia to trigger their contact mines. The lead horns several inches long contained a glass tube of bichromate solution that would break when bent and produce a chemical reaction, electrically detonating the explosive. A charge of 35-53 pounds of dynamite and later TNT made the uncontrolled contact mine a feared weapon. By 1907, the wide and successful use of sea mines led to an international convention at The Hague concerning the laying of automatic submarine contact mines. The Hertz detonator, in addition to persisting as a dependable device, has also exhibited the characteristic of being operable even after years of submersion. Some modern mines in the 21st century are equipped with horns similar to those of the 18th century design.

Naval Torpedo Station (Newport, Rhode Island 1869)

In 1869, Civil War Admiral David Porter (1813-1891), appointed by President Grant as assistant to the Secretary of the Navy, was instrumental in establishing under the Navy's Bureau of Ordnance (BuOrd) a new experimental Naval Torpedo Station (NTS) at Newport, Rhode Island. Porter's Civil War experience included mines and his plan for the new station involved hands-on experiments with torpedoes, mines, explosives, electrical devices to detonate them, and countermeasures to determine how the new technology should be used. He pushed for mines to be a high priority in the Navy and formed a Torpedo Corps within the Navy's Bureau of Ordnance. Initially Naval defense mines were the responsibility of NTS. The mine cases were an outside contract with all parts and fittings manufactured and assembled at the Station.[16]

The original site for NTS included former Army buildings on Goat Island in Newport harbor and buildings used by the Naval Academy at Newport during the Civil War. Until the mid-1880s, primary attention at the Station addressed understanding and improving the spar torpedo (mine) and the towed mine. Both mining and countermining

(MCM) were on the agenda of the original commanding officers at NTS.

Underwater use of electric lights to locate mines was examined, along with other ship self-protection measures. The underwater use of electric lights to spot mines was evaluated at NTS, and in 1884, the Navy ordered "torpedo searchlights" for installation on its new cruisers.[17]

Awareness and growing interest by the Navy in Whitehead's self-propelled torpedo, invented in 1866, placed new demands on NTS. After 1885, work on mines and MCM lessened and automobile torpedo efforts increased and became dominant. In the first years of the 1900s, all of the Navy's explosive development work at NTS was transferred to Indian Head, Maryland. Later in 1915, the manufacturing of naval defense mines moved from NTS to Philadelphia, Pennsylvania, and Norfolk, Virginia, leaving the torpedo and related technology at Newport. This may have been due to budgetary considerations as well as the assignment of defensive mine work to the Army beginning in the 1870s. The broad acceptance of the mobile torpedo and the continuing improvement of its performance and accommodating it on the various types of naval vessels placed additional space requirements on the facilities at the NTS.

Russia and Mine Warfare

European Countries observed the United States Confederacy's defensive mining successes during the Civil War and in 1875, Russia established a mine warfare school in St. Petersburg for the Baltic and Black Sea fleets. In 1877, the Russian Naval Academy at Nikolaiev instituted new courses on strategy and mine warfare. Hertz horn contact mines and electrically controlled observations mines provided coastal defense in the somewhat shallow Baltic approach to St. Petersburg in the Gulf of Finland and along the Black Sea coast near Odessa.

During the Russian-Turkish War, (1877-78), a superior Turkish Navy opposed the Russian on the Black Sea. With mines and Whitehead's torpedoes, Russia immobilized the Turkish opposition. This victory provided further proof of the efficacy of the mine as an important weapon in offensive warfare.[18]

United States Army Mines

The United States Congress recognized sea mines as a method of harbor and coast defense when submarine mining was added to the activities of the Engineering Corps of the Army. In 1871, General Abbot conducted mine experiments at Fort Totten, Willets Point, New York at the west end of Long Island Sound. Later, an experimental floating controlled minefield was planted in the Potomac River near Fort Washington, just south of Washington, DC. The 147 electrically-detonated mines were held in place 10 to 20 feet below the surface by 1000-pound anchors.

During the Spanish-American war in 1898, live mines were activated at the Potomac River installation. At this time, an attempt was made to develop a minefield for the New York harbor but failed due to poor condition of the equipment and a complete lack of technical knowledge. The laying of mines in harbors did not alleviate the safety concerns of the United States port cities. This situation continued through World War I and the U. S. Army was unable to plant any mines in the defense of the United States.[19]

During the nine month war (April 24, to December 10, 1898) the Spanish directed by Admiral Pascual Cervera effectively used electrically activated mines, the fort's guns, that overlooked the harbor at Santiago, Cuba, and log barriers. USN Captain William T. Sampson, acting Admiral in charge of the blockade of Cuba, was not able to enter the four-mile inlet leading into the port to attack the Spanish fleet.[20] The war exposed how limited were the U. S. Navy's mine warfare capabilities. Sea mines were still considered unconventional and not creatively used.[21]

Endnotes

[1] Source unknown

[2] Robert-Ian Salit, A Short History of Mine Sweeping. 4th International
    Symposium on Technology and the
Mine Problem, Naval Post Graduate School, Monterey, CA, March 12-
    16, 2000.

[3] Diana Schroeder, The History of the Sea Mine and its Continued
    Importance n Today's Navy"
    http://keyportmuseum.cnrnw.navy.mil/The_History_of_the_Sea_Mi
    ne.pdf

[4] Philip K. Lundeberg, *Samuel Colt's Submarine Battery, the Secret and
    the Enigma,* Smithsonian Institution Press, 1974, p.7

[5] John S. Cowie, *Mines, Minelayers and Minelaying,* London: Oxford
    University Press, 1949.

[6] Lt. J. N. Ferguson USN, The Submarine Mine, Naval Institute
    Proceedings, Vol. 40 Pt.2, Nov. Dec. 1914 p. 1698.

[7] James Tertius De Kay, *The Battle of Stonington: Torpedoes,
    Submarines, and Rockets in the War of 1812,* Naval Institute Press,
    Annapolis, MD, 1990, p. 7.

[8] Lundeberg, *op. cit.,* p. 3-6.

[9] ibid.„ p. 5.

[10] *ibid.,* p. 9.

[11] Counter countermeasures appeared in the 20th century.

[12] Ellsworth S. Grant, *The Colt Legacy: The Story of the Colt Armory in
    Hartford 1855-1900,* Providence,
RI, Mowbray Co., 1982.

[13] Detailed discussion of the impact of Confederate mines on then
    northern tactics and strategy is found in Admiral D. C. Porter,
    Torpedo Warfare. {*The North American Review.*/Volume 127, issue
    264, September-October 1878]
    http://www.thehunley.com/Torpedoo/o20Warfare.htm.

[14] Peggy Bottoms, http://maic.jmu.edu/journal/6.l/index.htrm#features.

[15] Gregory Hartman, *Weapons that Wait: Mine Warfare in the U. S.
    Navy,* Naval Institute Annapolis, MD, 1979, p 275

[16] W.J. Coggeshall, J. E. McCarthy, The Naval Torpedo Station Newport,
    Rhode Island 1658 through 1925, Newport Torpedo Station, 1944,
    Naval Underwater Warfare Systems Center, Newport, Rhode
    Island.

[17] www.exwar.org.

[18] Philip K. Lundeberg Undersea Warfare and Allied Strategy in World War I Part I: to 1916, Reprint from The Smithsonian Journal of History, Volume 1, No. 3, Autumn 1966, p. 4.

[19] www.geocities.com/fort_tilden/mine.html/

[20] http://www.exwar.org/Htm/8000PopH6.htm

[21] Albert B. Christman, *Naval Innovations 1776-1900*, Naval Surface Warfare Center, Dahlgren, Virginia, 1989, p. 363.

Sea Mines, the Submarine's Adversary and Weapon:

1775 to 1918

Part II: 20th Century

At the beginning of the new century, the relatively short Russo-Japanese War of 1904-05 brought naval encounters in the northern Pacific that proved costly in lives lost at sea and on land. Some of the losses were due to the defensive and offensive use of sea mines. It was a testing ground for sea mines against modern naval ships. Russian defensive mines prevented the Japanese from attacking Port Arthur, and the Japanese offensive use of mines impeded Russian ship movement to open seas.

Both sides as well as non-belligerents suffered severe losses from mines. In addition, there were self-losses by mining vessels. A further hazard from mines occurs when, due to storms or failure of mooring, the mines become adrift. Drifting mines as a danger continued throughout the century with hundreds of thousands planted in the various oceans.

This 19-month war focused attention to mines as an effective weapon, as can be seen by their broad use in successive wars at sea during the remainder of the 20th century. Previously, mines were placed in shallow water as an inshore weapon. In this war both sides used the mines in deep water. Russian mines were the cause of the largest number of Japanese ship losses.[22] The successful use of mines by the belligerents signaled mines had become an integral part of naval warfare.

Losses from Mines

Russian	Japanese
(Battleships)	(Battleships)
Petropavlosk sunk	*Hatuse* sunk
Pobieda, Sevastopol seriously damaged	*Yashima* sunk with crew
	Ashi, slightly injured
(Armored Cruiser)	(Coast Defense Ships)
Bayan seriously damaged	*Hei Yen, Sau Yen* sunk
(Cruiser)	(Cruisers)
Boyarine sunk with crew	*Akashi* seriously injured
	Myako, Takasago sunk

(Mine ship)	(Gunboat)
Yenissei sunk with crew (own mines)	*Kaimon* sunk
(Gunboats)	(Torpedo boat-destroyers)
Gremiatsky, Bobr, Otvagne sunk	*Hayatori, Akatuki* sunk
(Torpedo boat-destroyer)	(Torpedo-boats)
Vynoslow sunk	No. 8 and 48 sunk

The August 1905 peace negotiations held in Portsmouth, New Hampshire, and mediated by President Theodore Roosevelt resolved the conflict. There were additional impacts from the mines used during the war. Non-belligerent merchant ships were destroyed by mines adrift in the Yellow Sea because of poorly designed moorings or displaced by storms. It is interesting to note that no torpedo sinkings occurred during the war.

The Hague International Convention

With 44 nations participating, the Second Hague Peace Conference held from June until October of 1907 addressed the topic of sea mines. Increasing use of mines in wars from the middle of the 19th century and extensive use of mines during the Russo-Japanese War prompted the need for international regulation. Recognition of the efficacy and fear of sea mines is seen in Laws of War: Laying of Automatic Submarine Contact Mines (Hague VIII); October 18, 1907. Not all the participating nations had significant maritime interests. During the meetings, Great Britain was unsuccessful in convincing Germany and Russia to dispense with the use of mines altogether. This lack of agreement, especially between Great Britain and Germany, weakened the outcome of the Convention.

The Convention ended with thirteen agreed upon provisions. Articles one and five were clear and unequivocal. Austria-Hungry, Japan and the United States ratified the convention unconditionally; France and Germany ratified it except Article 2; Great Britain ratified with a declaration; and Greece, Italy, Portugal, Russia, Spain and the South American Republics did not ratify it at all.[23]

> **Article 1. It its forbidden-1 To lay unanchored automatic contact mines, except when they are to become harmless one hour at most after the person who laid them ceases to control them; 2 To lay anchored automatic contact mines which do not become harmless as soon as they have broken loose from their moorings; 3 To use torpedoes which do not become harmless when they have missed their mark.**

> Article 2, which forbids the laying of contact mines off the coast and the ports of the enemy, with the sole object of intercepting commercial shipping, is of limited value, for a belligerent has only to allege that mines were laid for a purpose other than merely intercepting commercial navigation.

> **Article 5. At the close of the war, the Contracting Powers undertake to do their utmost to remove the mines which they have laid, each Power removing its own mines.**
> **As regards anchored automatic contact mines laid by one of the belligerents off the coast of the other, their position must be notified to the other party by the Power which laid them, and each Power must proceed with the least possible delay to removed the mines in its own waters.**

It is of interest that in 1907, the significance of sea mines on both navy and commercial navigation was fully sensed. The Articles relating to mines were scheduled to be effective in January of 1910. A second Convention addressing mines was scheduled for 1914, the year that World War I started, with mines becoming a significant weapon. Difficult to enforce, the mine-related Articles had little impact on the development of mines and mine warfare.[24]

After World War I, the drifting contact mine was banned, even if it was occasionally used during World War II. The drifting mines were much harder to remove after the war, and they caused about as much trouble to both sides.

The agreements agreed upon at The Hague were largely unenforceable. From a military standpoint they were impractical if mining was to offer any tactical or strategic advantage. This is borne out by the actions of the belligerents during World War I, when conditions prevented enforcement. The stipulations of the original 1907 Hague Convention were never updated or amended. They remain, for all practical purposes, the basic international agreement on mine warfare in force today.

In summary, "The Hague Convention denied any warship the right to sink an unescorted merchant ship without first sending over a boarding party to decide if its cargo was contraband."[25]

Pre-World War I

At this juncture, US Navy mine warfare capability as a significant weapon was limited both in producing mines as well as mine laying and sweeping mines. Great Britain was the resource for mine development. One of the reasons for the lack of acceptance of mines at this time and continuing into the 20th century came from an 18th century perception of mines. As mines came into use, mine warfare was persistently perceived as a weapon for second-rate nations. It was not considered in line with traditional naval ways of fighting. Over time, this caused a continuing cyclic approach to supporting mines. In wartime, strong interest in all aspects of mines prevailed. Between wars, research, and attention lagged.

As a result of the successful mining in the Russo-Japanese War and the world-wide attention to the 1907 mining discussions at The Hague, the Navy requested Congress in 1907 for funds to convert certain cruisers of the *Baltimore* class (4500 tons, 20 knots) to mine depot ships. By June 1908, the *USS San Francisco* of this class was ordered refitted as a mine vessel and designated as a mine planter.

In 1909 with minimal ability to design and build mines, the U.S. Navy purchased the French-designed and -manufactured Sauter-Harle type designated as the US Naval Defense Mine Mark 2. This spherical mine with a contact inertia exploder and 175 pounds of guncotton came on the scene about 1909. Later in 1913, the French mine was used by the converted cruiser *USS San Francisco* in mine laying and sweeping practice operations. Several years later the *USS Baltimore* was modified and by 1915 conducted mining experiments in Chesapeake Bay and along the Atlantic coast. Later in 1918, the *USS Baltimore* operated as a minelayer for four months in the 250-mile long North Sea barrage between Norway and Scotland.

Technical and chronological details of the evolution of the United States Navy sea mines starting with Mark 1 is found in *Naval Weapons from 1883-to Present* (1982) by Norman Friedman.

Other countries were following somewhat similar courses of action for mine warfare. France adapted cruisers of its *Du Chalya* class (4000 tons, 20 knots). For mine warfare, England modified the three cruisers *Iphigenia*, *Alatona*, and *Thetis* (3600 tons, 18 knots). Each cruiser was fitted for carrying 100 mines.[26] Attention to countermeasures were also addressed by Germany, Great Britain, Italy and Austria in the years leading up to the World War I.

Germany was in the forefront of preparing for mine warfare by specially designing, building, and launching the mine depot ship *Pelikan* (2360 tons, 15 knots) in 1890. Similar German ships, the *Nautilus* and the *Albatross,* were launched in 1906 and 1907 (1970 tons, 20 knots). In 1910, Russia initiated the development of a minelayer submarine called the *Krab*, capable of carrying up to 60 mines, and commissioned in 1915. Performance of the mine-laying equipment did not meet expectations.

Germany's mine laying capability was such that two days after the start of the war, a minefield planted thirty miles off the English coast claimed a brand-new British cruiser. This and other success with mines and torpedoes is said to be attributable to the decade long thorough development and testing by Germany prior to the start of the war.[27]

Mine developments prior to World War I in Europe included initial investigation of the magnetic influence mine. Counter-sweeping devices included mine wire cutters, snags, and explosive moorings.

At the beginning of the war, the U.S. Navy adopted a Vickers mine, the British Elia, licensed from Italy. The mine was equipped with a mechanically-triggered contact consisting of a 3 foot long protruding float and required the target ships to be within a few feet of the mine to be effective. Because of this contact mine's distance limitation and overall lack of reliability, England's immediate response was to bring 7,500 Russian mines left over from the Russo-Japanese War from the Pacific to the North Sea.

Later in a retrospective article, in June of 1934, the Naval Institute Proceedings commented about the capability of British mines in the early part of World War I. "These (mines) were so defective that German submarines, when pursued, would seek a British mine field and hide under for protection from attacking surface craft." Mine range and reliability, both elusive requirements, were pursued in the wars of the 20th century.

In September of 1916, an unexploded German E Hertz horn exploder contact mine was safely towed to shore and used for experiment and redesign. Consequently the redesigned British mine called the H2 became available in late 1917 in numbers that permitted offensive mining in enemy waters.[28 29]

Subsequently, England used the first United States-designed mine, the Mark 5, a moored type with Hertz horns weighing and a total weight of 1500 pounds with 500 pounds of TNT. Although the range for damaging enemy shipping was increased it was not an optimum distance. The Mark 5 was long lived and still in use in World War II.

Dardanelles and Gallipoli

A strip of water 38 -mile long by ¾ to 1-mile wide is the access to Constantinople and the Black Sea from the Aegean Sea. In 1909, British war planning included strategies for taking control of the Dardanelles and having access to the Turkish capitol and beyond.

In the latter part of 1914, German Army officers and men assisted Turkey in fortifying the waterway with mines and howitzers and gun fortifications. It is of interest that the mines came from diverse sources. Russian mines found floating in the Bosporus were salvaged, refurbished and replanted. While French mines from Smyrna were also used. In addition, Bulgarian mines left over from the second Balkan War in 1913 were sown. With a total of about 300 mines, the defensive mine fields when completed along the Dardanelles included contact and shore detonated mines for miles across the waterway.

A British plan to take control of the waterway was put into operation in March 1915. It envisioned that a naval force would transit the Dardanelles. The intensive mining, combined with the shore batteries and mobile howitzers that could reach the minefields, brought the intrusion to a stalemate. British minesweeping was countered at night by the use of Turkish spotlights and enemy mine reseeding. An early Turkish mining of 20 mines sank the three British battleships *Ocean, Bouvet*, and *Irresistible.* In summary, the British battleships were kept at bay by mobile howitzers and the minefield batteries while the contact minefields blocked passage.[30] During the following ten months thousands of Allied troops tried unsuccessfully to advance using amphibious assaults along the Gallipoli peninsula with its awkward geography in a battle where relief, supplies or evacuation were impeded by the enemy mines and fortifications. With losses of more than 200,000 lives, British forces left in December. The total losses on both sides exceeded half a million. Integrated defensive mining was effective.

Germany's Mine Laying Submarines

During the War Germany constructed more than 350 submarines. The submarine minelayers are of interest. <u>Naval Institute Proceedings</u> November/December 1915 reported on German submarine mine layers with airtight chambers where mines, primarily contact type, are placed ready to be sown. A delayed rising mine was also used. The stowage chamber is flooded and the mines are released and sink. The 110-foot-long UC-5, an UC-1 type, was one of the 114 minelayers. In a 9-month period on 29 patrols, the UC-5 laid 200 mines and sunk 29 ships before it grounded and was scuttled. The UC-5's record was characteristic of the minelayers.

World War I German Mine Laying Submarines [31]

Type	Launch	Number	Mines	Crew
UC-1 Coastal Minelayer	1914-1916	15	12	14
UC-2	1915-1917	64	18	14
UC-3	1916-1918	16	14	32
UE-1 Ocean Mine Layer	1915-16	10	38	32
UE-2	1916-18	9	42	40

After the disaster at Gallipoli, Lord Herbert Kitchener, one of England's highly- ranked and important Army officers and a significant figure in the struggle on the Turkish peninsula, was dispatched in mid-1916 to go to Russia to encourage that country to persevere in its struggle with Germany. He was en route aboard the cruiser *HMS Hampshire* when the naval vessel struck a mine laid by a German submarine and sunk in ten minutes. Kitchener was drowned.

British Mine Laying Submarines

Between 1912-17, the Royal Navy constructed 58 E-class submarines capable of operating in blue water. Six were converted into mine layers. These submarines were responsible for sinking about 100 enemy ships of the German coast. Subsequently, they were used for mine laying in the English Channel. [32]

Responding to Mines

In late September 1914, weeks after the start of the War, England was taken aback by the loss of the three armored cruisers on the same day by a German submarine. This event and an increased sense of the danger from mines formalized England's War Orders on January 1, 1915 to take additional steps to be alerted to the presence of enemy submarines and mines. The orders provided prize money to trawlers and other vessels to report U-boat movements and participate in the capture or sinking of U-boats. Destruction of floating or moored enemy mines brought awards of £5 or £10. None of these measures proved effective.[33] Early enemy success with mines and submarines was not anticipated. Preparedness for countermining was lacking and in the case of the enemy submarine, there was no antisubmarine device to detect its presence when submerged.

Later in the war, the United States like England would have mines planted by U-boats along some of its seaports to interdict commercial shipping. The ports required mine clearing. As the war began the United States minesweeping force consisted of only three converted fleet tugs and a few fishing trawlers.[34] Eventually, defense involved ten tugs on permanent minesweeping. Later the force was augmented by lighter mine sweeping equipment on destroyers and torpedo boats.

After United States entry into the war, a steel net was sunk across the Verrazano Narrows between Brooklyn and Staten Island to keep German submarines out of the inner harbor. German submarines planted mines around Sandy Hook, and 16 tugboats based at Staten Island were turned into minesweepers. "Working in pairs, they swept the ocean every day for 100 miles out from Sandy Hook, finding and exploding a large number of floating mines."[35]

Germany's early, continuing, and expanding submarine successes shifted Allied naval efforts to a stronger defensive role. These efforts bought about the development and implementation of simple hydrophones for submarine detection along with TNT depth charges, sea mines, and, later in the war, broad convoying of merchant ships. Each contributed to eventual victory.

Sea Mines and the North Sea Barrage

Plans for mining the North Sea from Norway to the Orkneys, off Scotland, to deter the U-boats en route to the Atlantic were under consideration as early as 1915. In 1913, a British war plan considered mining the Heligoland Bight off Germany's North Sea coast and the Strait of Dover with 50,000 mines. This was dropped because of cost. The extreme merchant shipping losses brought it to the fore again in 1917. The ship losses for April 1917 escalated to 900,000 tons.

This was a very critical time, as the German submarine war against unprotected merchant shipping was succeeding. Ventures against the U-boats irrespective of the approach always demanded inordinate support including manpower, equipment, and financing. In the spring of 1917, two concepts, each a huge undertaking, were competing for immediate implementation and support. A consensus for greater support for merchant ship convoying to stem the U-boat was finally reached at this time. The barrage was also approved but with some restraint. Before long, the success of convoy enhancement became evident.

As planned the length of the barrage was 250 miles with a width of 15 to 20 miles. Initial estimate of the number of mines required as 120,000. This required number was substantially reduced with the development of the United States MK 6 (moored contact type mine), designed around a new galvanic firing device. Working at the Naval Torpedo Station in Newport, Rhode Island, Ralph C. Browne invented the mine's firing device.[36] The MK 6, in addition to Hertz horns, was equipped with two 70 foot vertical underwater antennas, one held above the mine by a float and the other the mooring cable below attached to the mine's anchor. Actual contact of the mine by the enemy vessel was not necessary. Contact by the U-boat with either of the mines vertical antennas produced galvanic action and initiated the explosion.

Enemy vessel contact with the Hertz horns provided an additional opportunity for an explosion.

The MK 6 vertical antennas above and below the mine substantially increased vertical and horizontal coverage and decreased the number of mines needed for a given area. Further, it did not require specialized minelayers and released mine layers for other assignments. The mine with 300 pounds of TNT was dropped from rails off the stern of surface vessel in water 30 to 3000 feet deep. Long-lived it was widely used from 1917 to about 1985. British mine planting began March and that of the United States in June of 1918 and continued on until October as the war was moving to an armistice. Large mine laying ships could lay 5,000 mines in a four-hour operation.[37] Cruisers *USS San Francisco* and *USS Baltimore* converted to mine laying were both assigned to the North Sea barrage and achieved laying thousands of mines in a few hours, Premature explosions of the MK 6 did not portend success. The United States contracted with automobile manufacturers to manufacture 6,000 mines a week. The United States produced, shipped and planted 56,611 mines and England planted 16,300. An estimate of the cost of the barrage in 1918 dollars was $40 million.[38]

The barrage is deserving of historical attention both as an important high-seas mining operation and an incredible engineering and logistical challenge achieved in a short time. However, as commented in 1966 by Philip K. Lundeberg, "it proved less than an unqualified success." Mine laying operations started in June 1918 (six months prior to the end of the War). Lack of performance may be attributed to the haste of mine development and manufacture and the results of the barrage on a longer war are unknown.

Another and darker view of the barrage and the uncertainty of its effects was presented by "Submarine Mining, Orphan Child of the Service" Naval Institute Proceedings, 1934. In addition to pointing out the Navy's cyclic interest in sea mines, the article raised questions regarding the barrage's overall viability. As noted above, the barrage was only completed a few months before the end of the war and its long-term capability was not tested. From the article:

> "It is a fact that only 43 percent of the mines were on duty when, after the war, the mine sweepers cleared the fields and this was only a matter of months after they were laid, whereas they should have stood guard for several years…who classed the venture as "a bluff that worked"".

Magnetic Mines

By 1918, British researchers developed and implemented the magnetic influence mine. The mine, the concrete-cased M-sinkers resting on the bottom, detonated when they sensed a ship's magnetic signature. A bottom location provided the necessary constant magnetic reference to be able to detect the presence of the magnetic steel hull of a vessel or submarine. Features of the magnetic mines included no requirement for a mooring cable. Further magnetic mines resting on the bottom were difficult to sweep. Magnetic mines introduced late in World War I needed further development. During the inter-war years, enhancements made them a better weapon and both sides in World War II widely and effectively used them.

With the war ending in the first year of deployment, 1918, and the poor reliability of the newly developed magnetic mine, the overall potential of the weapon was not fully understood or appreciated. In October of 1939 the First Sea Lord, Admiral Dudley Pound, wrote regarding the magnetic mine," It is really the limit that after knowing about magnetic mines since the last war, no practical method of dealing with them had been evolved."[39] During World War II degaussing (demagnetizing) ships was developed to reduce ship's magnetic signature and sensitivity to magnetic mines. This countermeasure provided relief at a cost of time and money ($300 million).

The Royal Navy in April 1918, laid early M-sinkers off Zeebrugge, Belgium on the North Sea in conjunction with an attempted destruction of the U-boat pens. The mining at Zeebrugge also involved the British H2 mentioned above an improved 1917 design based on an successful German contact mine configuration.[40] During 1918, 11 of the 31 U-boats lost by the Flanders flotillas were claimed by Channel minefields with a possible additional 11 losses from the same weapon.[41]

Use of magnetic mine is also cited in an article by Frank Reed Horton who wrote, "During the First World War, I served as an ensign in the United States Navy aboard a minesweeper in the North Sea. Our ship and its partner exploded more than 1,000 magnetic mines." Magnetic mines, in use late in World War I and requiring improvement, improved during the inter-war years and were widely and effectively used as an important weapon by both sides in World War II.[42]

Summary

At the time of the Armistice in November of 1918, the mine was a comparatively inexpensive weapon with a proven success in naval warfare. The mine was responsible for the highest attrition of warships, compared with that of all other surface weapons combined in that war. In World War I, more than 300,000 mines sank or damaged more than 950 Allied and Central Power, warships, merchantmen, and submarines[43]

Allies lost 586 merchant ships and 87 warships not including 152 small patrol boats and minesweepers. The Central Powers' losses to mines included 129 warships, excluding an unknown number of merchant ships and submarines. Once again, the total ship damage in WWI from mines was far greater than that by gunfire and torpedoes[44]

The effectiveness of the submarine, the torpedo, and the mine almost from the first days of World War I was not anticipated. Countering each became an all-consuming task for both sides for the entire war. In the almost 90 years since the Armistice, means to counter the submarine and the two weapons continues to confound those involved.

A kind of consensus regarding the lack of preparation or anticipation of the submarine's *guerre de course,* the mine, and torpedo in some instances was based on the lack of fiscal resources in peacetime to meet the requirements of the military. In the case of Great Britain, attention to preparing for offensive high seas battleship or dreadnought encounter seems to have precluded adequate support for alternative weapons like the mine and torpedo. Throughout the war, the inexpensive mine inhibited battleship maneuvers or even putting to sea in some instances.[45]

Historical evidence shows that sea mines, depth charges and submarines at some point in their introduction received slow acceptance as they were perceived as being a weapon for nations with small or inferior navies. In the 19th century, acceptance of steam versus sail in the United States Navy was not unanimous.

During most of the first half of the 20th century, the concentration on capital-ship construction with the attendant cost and crew size was often steep competion for small ship needs and attention to new naval technologies. In retrospect, small-specialized ships for convoys, mining and countermining were frequently lacking. However, the role of mines in World War II, the Korean War, the Vietnam War, and the Iraq Wars have each brought careful attention to sea mines and their defensive and offensive roles as the weapons that wait.

World War I 230-mile long sea mine barrage[*]

*http://www.globalsecurity.org/...icy/navy/nrtc/14152 pdf_chl

Endnotes

[22] www.exwar.org/htm/800htm.

[23] Ferguson, *op. cit.,*p. 1703.

[24] The Avalon Project, Source d. Shindler and j. Toman, *The Laws of Armed Conflict*, Martinus Nihjoff Publisher, 1988, pp. 804-807.

[25] Len Deighton, *Blood, Tears, and Folly: An Objective Look at World War ll*, Harper Collins Publishers, 1993, p. 13.

[26] Philip R. Alger USN, (translation from Le Yacht) The Employment of Submarine Mines in Future Wars, Naval Institute Proceedings, September 1908, Volume 34 No. 3, p. 1040.

[27] Richard Alexander Hough, *The Great War at Sea*, Oxford University Press, NY, 1983 p. 48.

[28] *Ibid.* p. 264.

[29] Philip K. Lundeberg Undersea Warfare and Allied Strategy in World War I Part II: 1916-1918, Reprint from The Smithsonian Journal of History, Volume 1, No. 3, Autumn 1966, p. 67.

[30] Hough, *op. cit.*, p. 155.

[31] uboat..net.

[32] www.exwar.org.

[33] Willem Hackman, *Seek and Strike,* Her Majesty's Printing Office, London, 1984, p, 11,12.

[34] David A. Morris LCDR, U.S. Navy, The Mine Cycle: History, Indications, and Future, http://www.globalsecurity.org/military/library/report/1997/Morris.htm.

[35] http://www.geocities.com/fort_tilden/uboats.html.

[36] Lundeberg, *op, cit.,* p. 64. A. B. Feuer, *The U.S. Navy in WW I: Combat at Sea and in the Air,* Praeger, Westport, Ct, 1999, p. 16

[37] Paul G. Halpern, *A Naval History of World War I,* Naval Institute Press, Annapolis, MD, 1994, p. 439

[38] *Ibid.* p. 440.

[39] Correlli Barnett, *Engage the Enemy more Closely: The Royal Navy in the Second World War,* Norton, New York, 1991, p. 91.

[40] Lundeberg, *op. cit.*, p. 67.

[41] Hough, op. cit., p. 264.

[42] http//www.exwar.org/Htm/8000PopJ2.htm.

[43] Morris, *op, cit.,* p, 7.

[44] Gregory K. Hartman, *Weapons that Wait: Mine Warfare in the U. S. Navy,* Annapolis, MD., Naval Institute Press, 1979, p. 15.

[45] Hough, *op.*

"Unlikely Allies:

Great, Britain, France,

The U.S. and Japan in WWI"

Introduction

When World War I broke out in Europe on August 4, 1914, Great Britain declared war against Germany. At first, the British assumed that Japan would remain neutral. Several days later, Great Britain asked Japan for naval assistance against the Imperial German Fleet in the Pacific. Participation by Japan would be in compliance with a provision of the then current Anglo-Japanese Alliance. Two weeks after the start of the World War, on August 24, 1914, Japan's naval support of Great Britain began in the Pacific Ocean with a Japanese declaration of war against Germany.

The roots for Great Britain's the request were established in a highly secret nine months period of negotiations in 1901-02 between these island maritime nations. The new Anglo-Japanese Alliance was officially accomplished January 30, 1902 with a public announcement in February. Prior to promulgation, the Alliance was shown to Washington (a silent partner). An Alliance benefit was that it would help maintain an "open door" to the Orient.1

One part of Japan's initial participation involved an almost immediately successful joint sea and land attack with Great Britain against the important German Yellow Sea port and naval base on leased land at Tsingtao on the Shantung Peninsula. The action ended on November 7, 1914. Other elements of Japan's naval advocacy during the following four years included assistance in the Pacific and Indian oceans. It is a bit surprising that in 1917-18, Japanese destroyers fought German and Austro-Hungarian submarines in the Mediterranean. Japan's support for the Allies came in other ways as well. In 1916, Japan delivered thirty-four trawlers to France. The following year, in five months[2]

Japanese shipyards built 12 *Kaba* class destroyers for France. This is the first example of a European power using Japanese industry on a large scale.[3]

Why did Great Britain enter into an Alliance with Japan?

This diplomatic move was a first in several respects. It was the first full-scale alliance with any nation by Great Britain in almost a century. In the new century, Great Britain found itself in financial straits as a result of the thirty-two month war with the Boers in South Africa and in the beginnings of a naval race with France and Germany. Pre-war naval emphasis on capital ships (dreadnoughts) by the primary naval powers placed a limit on the availability of cruisers and other naval ships that proved to be better suited to the type of naval warfare that evolved in the 1914-18 war.

According to naval historian Arthur J. Marder, "…from 1901-02 Admiralty looked upon Germany as the potential enemy of the Royal Navy."[4] Further, France and particularly Russia were presumed to have designs on parts of the Far East critical to Great Britain's interests. A global British Empire and a sometimes-extended Royal Navy could use support from a country with a proficient navy and strong maritime interests. Japan with success in the Sino-Japanese War (1894-95) and gaining as an economic power looked for assurance in holding the gains that it had made in Manchuria and Korea as result of that war. An alliance with Great Britain offered advantages. A further alignment in diplomatic arrangements was the 1904 agreement between England and France that resolved their antagonisms and controversies but was not an alliance.[5]

The initial Anglo-Japanese Alliance allowed that in the event of Japan at war with Russia, Great Britain would remain neutral. Great Britain would intervene if a second power came to Russia's aid. Containment of Russian power and maintaining an "open door" policy for China trade were principal goals. The Russo-Japanese war followed shortly after the signing of the Alliance. The war required Russia to move a substantial part of its coal-burning fleet 20,000 miles from the Baltic to the northern Pacific Ocean. The Alliance partnership precluded Russian ships from coaling ashore on the voyage from the Baltic.[6]

The Alliance was renewed, on August 12, 1905, just prior to Japan's victory over Russia and the signing of the peace at Portsmouth, New Hampshire. The Alliance deliberations at the renewal included participation by the Alliance partners in the event of a single power attack on one of the partners. Further, there was acknowledgement of Japan's interest in Korea. Discussion by the Alliance partners included consideration of appropriate action in the event of a probe by Russia into northwest India. By 1907, France, Russia, Japan and Great Britain shared common goals. In 1910, there was British support for Japan's goals in Manchuria.

On July 13, 1911, the third Alliance treaty was signed in London. It renewed and extended the Alliance. At this point, the needs of the participants were divergent on some issues. One of Great Britain's foremost interests pertained to the security of the Pacific Ocean area dominions of Australia and New Zealand. There were policy differences regarding China. Japan looked for protection against the fear of isolation in the Pacific vis-à-vis the United States. This version of the alliance excluded America from the nations that Britain would fight on Japan's side.[7] This last Alliance renewal provided a basis for Japan's eventual war declaration three years later.

At a May 1911 British ministerial meeting in London prior to the ten-year Alliance extension with Japan, a hypothetical case of a discontinuance of the Alliance with Japan in 1914 was considered. Foreign Secretary Sir Edward Grey, presented the following statement: "…in the interest of strategy, in the interest of naval expenditure, and in the interests of stability, it is essential that the Japanese Alliance be extended."* It appears prescient that the year 1914 was provided as an example.

Japan's disposition regarding the four-year war with Germany is clouded. At various points during the War, there seems to have been a reluctant willingness to participate. When participation did occur, it was effective and did help the Allied cause.

In the years leading up to the war, diplomacy and treaty building were not the singular concern of nations with substantial navies. It was a period of rapidly changing and improving technology of the fighting ships including their construction, capability and weaponry. Further, advancement in the development, manufacture, and improvements in naval guns, mines, depth charges, submarines, and torpedoes provided additional challenges to the countries' naval tacticians and naval strategists. Technological advancements brought increased skill requirements for the men manning the ships and as previously mentioned, fiscal limitations were omnipresent. Many challenges were to be encountered and at the same time occasions occurred for errors to be made. It is pertinent to mention that the primarily coal-burning naval warships were a huge encumbrance for the navy planners, strategists, and tacticians at all times.

----

*Arthur J. Marder, *From the Dreadnought to Scapa Flow, The Royal Navy in the Fisher Era, The Road to War,* Vol.1, Oxford University Press, London, 1961, p. 238

Pre-war British Naval Position

Great Britain concentrated its fleet in home waters, not for home islands protection but to prevent German cruisers from breaking out into the oceans and trade routes. This period also saw a reduction in the Royal Navy's Mediterranean and China squadrons and termination of the South Atlantic force. As early as 1905, the Admiralty slowly moved toward a policy of recalling the Mediterranean fleet in time of war, first under some contingencies and then under most.[8] Fiscal and naval manpower considerations helped foster the reductions. Manpower for the growing navies of the competing powers of Great Britain and Germany as also a priority. It happened that England maintained its navy with volunteers while Germany used conscription to fulfil its quotas. As mentioned above, the manpower sought now had an additional need: competence in technological areas.

Under these conditions, naval support for Great Britain around the globe came from good relations with the United States providing a naval backup in the western Atlantic as well as in the Pacific. France provided important naval coverage in the Mediterranean with the 1904 Entente mentioned above.[9]

Japan Enters the War

Japan quickly accepted the naval role of protecting Britain's interests in the Pacific as the War started. Initially, Japan's viewpoint made it clear that the ground war was a European event and not in the sphere of interest for the Japanese Army. However, by February of 1916 a willingness to send troops to the West was stated. In some instances the expression *willing reluctance* may have been appropriate. The record shows that in addition to naval support for the Allied cause Japanese support included arms, industrial products, shipyards, and merchant ships.

"On August 15, Japan, acting with the advice and consent of Great Britain, sent an ultimatum to Germany demanding the immediate withdrawal of German warships from the Orient and surrender to Japan of the leased territory of Kiauchau (Shantung Peninsula)."[10] With no response from Germany, Japan declared war on August 23. The remainder of the year saw Japanese naval action mainly in two different areas. One was (as previously mentioned) the immediate joint action with components of the British Navy in the siege at Tsingtao on the Yellow Sea. The other direct action was to take Germany's Pacific Micronesia islands. Before the end of the year both were successful.

Germany in the Pacific

Germany was well established on China's Shantung Peninsula. Sino-German commercial collaboration on the Shantung Peninsula and German acquisition for 99 years of Kiauchau, a 200-square mile area, dated from 1897. In the following years, Tsingtao, Germany's only fortified base in foreign waters, included a German-style city, industrial and maritime facilities, and substantial fortifications on the bay.

By 1914, German holdings in the Pacific also included the Mariana, Marshall, Caroline, New Guinea, Samoa, and Solomon Islands distributed on both sides of the equator and mostly west of the 170° longitude line.

At the time of Japan's declaration of war against Germany, the Shantung German industrial and military garrisoning was significant. Total troops numbered about 6,000, and naval support included an Austro-Hungrian armed cruiser, five gunboats and two destroyers.

Germany's East Asiatic Squadron under the leadership of Vice Admiral Maximilian Graf von Spee, equipped with the new armored cruisers *Scharnhorst* and

Gneisenau plus three light cruisers, was the challenge to the British in the Pacific. Normally based in Tsingtao, von Spee in a pre-war move by July 17 removed his armored cruisers from the Shantung region to the Caroline Islands. The Admiral's plan was to impact British trade routes by operating off the West Coast of South America with coaling capability at Chilean ports. Intelligence regarding the location of naval vessels of both sides in remote oceanic areas was frequently incorrect or not available.

Japan's late August entry in the war with a clear naval superiority in the Pacific motivated Admiral von Spee's disposition of his forces. This is exemplified in the light cruiser *Emden's* November 9 assignment to the Indian Ocean. After three months of successful encounters, the *Emden* was sunk off the Cocos Islands in the Indian Ocean by the Australian light cruiser *Sydney*. The *Emden's* successes during that period included sinking or capturing seventeen British merchant ships of 68,000 tons in the North Pacific and Indian Oceans. During these early months of the war, Germany's East Asiatic Squadron was gradually decimated.

In addition to sinking and capturing ships of British registry, two significant open sea battles occurred in the next several months. These battles have been noted as the last open sea battles of the 20th Century fought without sea mines, submarines and airplanes. The first was the clash between mostly light and heavy German and British cruisers off Coronel on the coast of Chile on November 1, 1914. This was a decided victory for the Germans. Two of the four of the participating British men-of-war were lost with no German ship losses. This was the first naval battle loss by the British in one hundred years.

On December 8, a second sea battle of armed cruisers occurred in the South Atlantic at the Falkland Islands with the *Dresden* escaping and the other six German ships sunk.

Von Spee was lost with his flagship-armored cruiser *Scharnhorst.* His two sons were also lost in the battle. Even with a much-reduced German cruiser capability in the Pacific and Indian Oceans, there was a contributing naval role for Japan throughout the war.

Tsingtao

Upon declaration of war against Germany with China in a neutral status, Japan, with a strong interest in the German holdings on the Shantung Peninsula, immediately authorized a blockade of Tsingtao. The New York Times on August 17, 1914, headlined the beginnings of the assault with 16,000 Japanese troops embarking for the Yellow Sea stronghold and included a map of the area. The following three-month siege of the long-held and well-established German stronghold ended with the German surrender on November 7. Land and sea forces were primarily Japanese. Other Western Allied participation was minimal with British naval support and troops, South Wales Borderers and the 36th Sikhs from the Tientsin Hong Kong Garrison.

Twelve forts and barracks for 5000 troops protected Tsingtao and environs, considered the Kaiser's stronghold in the Far East. It was also identified as the "German Gibraltar of the East."[11] At the time of the Japanese assault, several thousand additional support troops were added. The Japanese naval assault and landings with 60,000 troops, including British participation, began in early September. The extensive bombardment included both land and naval encounters. A German-Austro-Hungarian surrender occurred November 7.

Wakamiya Sea Plane Tender

A Japanese trading ship, *Wakamiya,* modified as a seaplane tender and equipped with 4 Farman floatplanes, entered service in 1913. During September at Tsingtao, *Wakamiya*'s seaplanes (with a speed of 60 mph and ceiling of 1500 feet) participated in a great number of sorties, dropped bombs, and provided observations. Pilots used visual communications with each other. Even with the limitations of the aircraft involved at that time, the value of aerial observation at sea and other capabilities of planes in naval warfare did not go unnoticed.

German Pacific Islands

Historians, considering Japan's objectives as an ally, identify taking possession of the German holding in China's Shantung region and the various German Micronesian islands as a primary goal. The successful siege of Tsingtao was consummated with the German surrender on November 7, 1914. Almost immediately (January 18, 1915) Japan submitted 21 demands to China regarding Japanese claims. The Sino-Japanese treaty of May 25, 1915, allowed Japan rights in southern Manchuria, eastern Inner Mongolia and Germany's economic holdings on the Shantung Peninsula.

Even more quickly within two weeks of declaring war against Germany, German colonial possessions north of the equator in the Pacific surrendered to Japan. The Mariana Islands, Caroline Islands (East), Caroline Islands (West), and the Marshall Islands were captured and occupied by the Japanese on about October 6, 1914. Resolution of Japanese long-term entitlement to these islands and clarification of eventually returning the Shantung region to China were resolved at the 1919 Peace Conference.

Japanese Naval Role 1915-1916

Immediate opportunities for Japanese naval support included assisting in the search for Germany's remaining battle cruisers in the Pacific and Indian Oceans. Japan also provided convoy assistance to the vast movement of Australian and New Zealand troops and war materials across the Indian Ocean. With a reduced British naval presence, especially in the north Pacific, as well as a lessening of German capability, Japan's naval presence became significant. Japan's occupation of the northern German Micronesian islands also caused concern and discomfiture with the British dominions of Australia and New Zealand. This concern presented itself later at the peace negotiations in France.

Singapore Indian Troop Mutiny 1915

January and February of 1915 saw unrest within the Indian Army in India and abroad. Planned army uprisings at Rangoon, Burma, in January of 1915 and February of 1915 at Lahore, India were aborted. At Singapore on February 15, the 5th Light Infantry Battalion of 800 (all Punjabi Muslims), plus 100 members of the Malay States Guides Mule Battery mutinied.

Causes for the mutiny included the prospect of the battalion being assigned to fight Muslim Turkey. Later examination of the motivation for mutiny included poor leadership, inadequate rations, and poor NCO promotion prospects. Pan-Muslim feelings were also considered to have contributed to the mutiny.[12]

On Singapore Island, there were 231 regular European troops. Thirty-two British soldiers and civilians were killed. German prisoners were released, a few fled. Within ten days the insurrection was subdued, the support coming from marines and crews from British, French, Russian and Japanese warships in port. Several hundred civilians also were involved in the suppression of the mutiny. On February 17, two protected Japanese cruisers *Tsushima* and *Otowa* landed marines in the action. It has been mentioned that about 100 Japanese marines and sailors came ashore to assist.[13]

Mediterranean Submarine Warfare 1917-18

By the middle of April 1917, the adversaries within the confines of the Mediterranean in the anti-submarine war included Great Britain, Italy and France aligned against Germany and Austria-Hungry. Italy, neutral since August 3, 1914 gave up its neutral status and declared war against Austria-Hungry in 1915 and Germany in August 1916.

Germany's late 1916 movement toward reinstitution of unrestricted submarine warfare proved to be highly successful as the new year opened. With a total of 150 U-boats engaged in unrestricted warfare, the Feburary and March 1917 total overall tonnage lost to the U-boats was on track for an Allied disaster by fall of that year. Further, the exchange ratio the number of Allied ships sunk to the number of submarines lost reached 167 per U-boat by April, a fivefold increase from the February exchange ratio of 53 per U-boat. Overall, 25 % of the total British shipping loss during the War from mines and submarines occurred in the Mediterranean. Further, 7% of the total sinkings of the War took place in April 1917.[14] In spite of historical evidence favorable to convoying, the Allies in World War I waited nearly three years until April 1917 to invoke convoy as a way to effectively curb the very successful U-boat sinking of merchant ships. It was under these near-crisis loses from the U-boats that Great Britain requested Japan's naval support in the Mediterranean. More than one request was required to have a Japanese naval presence in the European Theater. Japan surmised that sending a fleet would leave the Pacific open to expansion of American naval power.[15]

The United States as a recent entrant into the war did not have a presence in the Mediterranean until 1918. By then, with the war winding down, there were thirty-six United States newly constructed 110-foot wooden submarine chasers operating out of Corfu and an additional 18 assigned at Gibraltar.

Japanese Naval Presence in the Mediterranean 1917-18

On February 16, 1917, Great Britain advised Japan that in a post war environment, it would agree to Japan's claims to German rights in Shantung and possessions in the islands, of the Marshall, Caroline and Marianas Archipelagos, north of the equator. Australian rights to the German areas south of the equator were part of the agreement. This secret agreement also had assurance from the Russian, French, and Italian governments. Perhaps this agreement ended Japan's slow and reluctant response to Great Britain's request for help in the Mediterranean. At the 1919 Peace Conference at Versailles, this concession was granted with the exception that the date and conditions for the return of the Shantung area to China was not specified.

Mid-April 1917, a Japanese Mediterranean squadron of destroyers began to assemble at Malta to assist to the Allied fighting against the German and Astro-Hungarian U-boats. The Japanese destroyers, initially 12, with cruiser flagships were an important part of the anti-submarine convoy escort.[16] Destroyers were needed to hunt submarines or provide escort for the now heavily invoked convoy system. Marder's comment regarding destroyer performance in the Mediterranean points out the efficiency of the dozen Japanese destroyers.[17]

Destroyers: Time at Sea

Japan	British	French/Italian
72 %	60 %	~45 %

In June 1917, in recognition of the Japanese ship handling skills, the British transferred to Japan for duration the *Acorn* (H) class destroyers *HMS Nemesis (Kanran) and HMS Minstrel (Sendan)*. The ships were returned in 1919. This brought the number of Japanese destroyers in the Mediterranean to fourteen. Marder in <u>From the Dreadnaught to Scapa Flow</u> points out the seriousness of some of Japan's destroyer captains, "So impregnated with a sense of duty that some of their destroyer captains committed hara-kiri when a U-boat sank a ship they were escorting!"[18]

May 3, 1917

On this date, the British troopship *Transylvania,* an ex-Cunard ship, departed Marseilles bound for Alexandria with about 200 officers and 2,860 troops. The Japanese destroyers *Matsu* and *Sakaki* escorted the ship. On the following day in the Gulf of Genoa, the German submarine U-63 torpedoed the *Transylvania.*

During passenger offloading to the *Matsu,* the *Sakaki* attempted to force the U-boat to remain submerged. A second torpedo from the U-63 caused the *Transylvania* to sink more rapidly. One of the destroyers saved 1,000 of the survivors. Other vessels came to assistance, but most of the survivors were aboard the Japanese ships. In all, 414 passengers lost their lives.[19] Later the *New York Times* reported that during the rescue effort, a second torpedo struck and "blew the ship sky high."[20]

June 11, 1917

"Japanese Destroyer Damaged, while Japanese destroyers were attacking a submarine in the Mediterranean on June 11, the destroyer *Sakaki* was torpedoed and damaged, says an official announcement of the Japanese Admiralty June 15. The damaged craft was towed to port.

The Japanese Naval attaché in London announced the loss of 55 lives aboard the *Sakaki*. –N.Y. Herald, 17,6." [21]

Other references identify source of the torpedoing that destroyed the bow of the *Sakaki* with a loss of 68 of the 92-person crew as the German designed Austrian submarine U-27. The destroyer was on escort duty off Crete in the eastern Mediterranean. The destroyer was salvaged and repaired. Shortly after this incident the U-27, a 121-foot submarine with a crew of 30 at sea for 90 days, traveled 4200 miles on the surface and 70 miles submerged in the eastern Mediterranean and evaded, attacked, and sank a number of ships.

To help place the scale of Japanese participation in perspective, by early 1917 Allied vessels against submarines in the Mediterranean included 147 destroyers, 75 torpedo boats, 200 trawlers, 68 submarines, 78 sloops, gunboats and other craft.[22]

Halpern in *Naval War in the Mediterranean* (1987) noted Japanese destroyer support: "The Japanese were largely responsible for escorting troopships, in fact the postwar study by the Mediterranean Staff concluded that without the assistance of the Japanese forces 'the situation would have been impossible'."[23]

United States and Japan Relationship

Japan's naval role of assisting Great Britain was extended to the United States with President Wilson's declaration of war in April of 1917. Throughout the war an attitude of suspicion towards Japan and its goals was held by some in United States and Great Britain. With exceptions, an air of diffidence seems to have been detected in many quarters of the governments when dealing with Japan. The incident of the Zimmerman Telegram and the United States policy regarding immigration of Japanese during the remaining years of the war provided a source of continuing diplomatic difficulties.

One of the immediate benefits from Japanese naval coverage in the Pacific was that it allowed the United States to move naval forces from the Pacific to directly aid the British. The agreement between the American and Japanese government made it possible for the United States to withdraw ships from the Philippines and from the Western Pacific as those waters were protected by Japanese vessels. The Japanese warships patrolled the Pacific Ocean from Japan to Manila, then to Honolulu, and as far south as the South Sea Islands.[24]

Summary

In the final years of the War, Japan was requested to provide more naval assistance in the European Theater. The response mentioned that Japan was already in the Pacific Ocean, Indian Ocean, Australian waters, the Mediterranean, and in 1918 in Vladivostok. Earlier requests of the Japanese included solicitations for purchase of a modern Japanese battleship that are refused.

The primary reason for the Anglo-Japanese Alliance stemmed from a British need for naval support in parts of the Pacific Ocean to counter German naval capabilities in that region. Japan fulfilled that requirement and more. With the end of the war, the 1919 Peace Conference in Paris and the January 1920 Treaty of Versailles legitimized the wartime Japanese land expansion and initiated Japan's acceptance as a world power. The German islands in the Pacific north of the equator were mandated to Japan with virtual sovereignty.[25] At this time, the Japanese Navy was third in the world.

The Peace Conference also established the League of Nations to work toward and implement international security to preclude conflict. During the negotiations for the League, Japan proffered a clause in the League's covenant that would prohibit racial discrimination. It was rejected.

Japan's participation in the war, although important and in some ways critical, was small in comparison with other warring nations from the viewpoints such as manpower involved, manpower and civilian losses and cost. Consequently, the participation of Japan on the side of the Allies is not frequently cited in historical writings about World War I. It is for this reason that the purpose of this article is to bring attention to some of the events demonstrating Japan's role.

Anglo-Japanese Alliance Ends

The Washington Conference (1921-22) also known as the International Naval Conference on Naval Limitation included the signing on December 13, 1921 of the Four-Power Treaty between Great Britain, France, Japan and the United States. It provided that all the signatories would be consulted in the event of a controversy between two of them over "any Pacific Question"[26], and a pledge to respect each other's rights in their island possessions in the Pacific. The replacing of the 1911 Anglo-Japanese Alliance by the new agreement was considered a major accomplishment.[27]

Endnotes

[1] Ernest W. Clement, *A Handbook of Modern Japan,* A. C. McClury & Co. Chicago, 1907, 157.

[2] Timothy D. Saxon, "Anglo-Japanese Naval Cooperation, 1914-1918", Naval War College Review, Winter 2000, p. 14; Saxon provides a thorough treatment of the Japanese participation,

[3] Paul G. Halpern, *The Naval War in the Mediterranean 1914-1918,* Naval Institute, Annapolis, MD, 1987, p. 258.

[4] Arthur J. Marder, *From the Dreadnought to Scapa Flow,* Vol. 1 *The Road to War, 1904-1914,* London: Oxford University Press, 1961, p. 40.

[5] Hew Strachan, *The First World War: Volume 1 To Arms,* Oxford University Press, 2001, p. 14.

[6] Stephan Howarth, *The Fighting Ships of the Rising Sun: The Drama of the Imperial Japanese Navy1895-1945,* Atheneum, NY, 1983, p. 82

[7] Ibid., p. 117

[8] Halpern, op, cit., p. 12

[9] Strachan, op, cit., p. 442

[10] European War Notes, Naval Institute Proceedings, 1914 v, p. 1557

[11] Saxon, op, cit., p. 6

[12] Strachan, op, cit., p. 797

[13] www,naval-history,net/WW1NavyJapanese.htm)

[14] Saxon, op, cit., p. 17

[15] Hew Strachan (editor), *World War I: A History,* Oxford University Press, 1998, p. 181

[16] http://www.navalhistory.net/WW1NavyJapanese.htm, p. 1.

[17] Arthur J. Marder, *From the Dreadnought to Scapa Flow, The Royal Navy in the Fisher Era 1904-1919, Victory and Aftermath (January 1918- July 1919),* Vol. V, Oxford University Press, New York, 1970, p. 36.

[18] Ibid, p. 37.

[19] http://www.harboro.ndirect.co.uk/rayworth.htm

[20] New York Times, May 26, 1917, p. 3:8

[21] Naval Institute Proceedings vol. 43, #7. (whole 173), July 1917, p. 1616.

[22] Arthur J. Marder, *From the Dreadnought to Scapa Flow, The Royal Navy In the Fisher Era, 1917: Year of Crisis,* Vol. 4, Oxford University Press, New York, 1969, p. 95

[23] Halpern, op, cit., p. 388.

[24] New York Times, January 2. 1918, p. 11:5

[25] Ian Gow, *Military Intervention in Pre-War Japanese Politics,* RoutledgeCurzon, London, 2004, p. 77

[26] Encyclopedia Britannica, Fifteenth Edition 1990, 12:510:2a.

[27] Lawrence H. Douglas, "The Submarine and The Washington Conference", Naval War College Review, March-April 1974, p. 96.

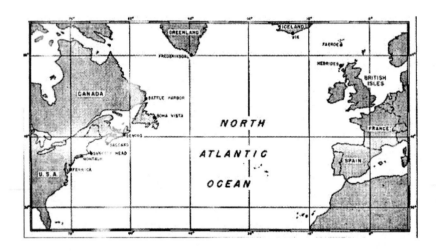

Loran Stations North Atlantic 1942-43

LORAN

Showing the Way: Long Range Navigation
(Land, Sea, Air)

Part I 1940-1942

Loran, a World War II navigation system fulfilling wartime all weather needs with a near global coverage and importance to the war effort, was devised, tested, and broadly implemented within a period of less than four years. The destruction of Allied ships in the North Atlantic gave rise to the crash program to create the navigation system. It is still a system of importance in the new century.

This paper addresses the question, "Why and how did Loran happen?" To this end, background, events, and highlights are examined during the twenty-four months of research and development preceding the official transfer of the system to the Navy on January 1, 1943.

Loran was a concept and proposal in late 1940; the investigative system research was virtually completed by September 1941.[1] In 1942, the first Loran system operating at 1950 kHz was in use along the Northeast Atlantic Coast, providing long distance ship and aircraft navigation.

Extensive system implementation started in 1943. At the end of the war in 1945 at least 75,000 receivers and 100 transmitters were installed and 2,500,000 Loran charts distributed to all services. The charts from the Navy Hydrographic Office included fifty million square miles of the earth's surface.[2] About 70 stations had been installed, offering nighttime service over 30 percent of the surface of the earth, principally the most trafficked Atlantic waterways and nearly the entire Pacific. Up to July 1945, $71,000,000 worth of Loran equipment was delivered to the services.[3]

After World War II

Loran was one of the three original projects[4] at the MIT Radiation Laboratory sponsored in 1940 by the National Defense Research Committee (NDRC). In the years following WWII, development continued under the aegis of the United States Coast Guard (USCG), to provide air, land and sea navigation for the military, for maritime interests and for the airline industry. The Korean, Vietnam, and Cold Wars again gave opportunity for Loran use in a variety of geographical areas. Technological advances involving satellites and missiles arose in the late 1950s, requiring navigational needs that were met with Loran C operating in the VLF spectrum (100kHZ). The Navstar/GPS system would later employ Loran's method of using time difference in the arrival of radio signals to calculate position.

Loran's Relevance in 2005

More than sixty years after Loran beginnings, the navigation system is still worldwide with additional potential value in the future to meet new needs. This is substantiated in an article appearing in the European Journal of Navigation in December 2003 asking "Is Loran-C the answer to GPS vulnerability?"

"Loran's Capability to Mitigate the Impact of GPS Outage on GPS Position, Navigation, and Time Applications" is the title of a December 2004 evaluation of eLoran (enhanced Loran) to address GPS backup. The article represents the findings of industrial and government organizations.

Concept

The Loran system allows a vessel or aircraft to determine its position in all weathers and at great distances from shore. A radio wave is sent from a master station and received by the ship or plane and slave stations. On receipt of the pulse, the slave sends out its pulse, which is also received by the vessel or plane. The ship or plane Loran receiver-indicator measures electronically the difference in time of arrival of the radio waves from a ground station.

Using Loran charts for the area served by the ground stations, a line of position is determined from the time difference. A second line of position is determined from another "pair" of stations. The intersection of the two lines provides a "fix.[5]

Measuring the time of arrival of radio waves aboard a ship, aircraft, or fixed shore station immediately created an additional and diverse number of new challenges regarding how radio waves propagate over the various signal paths as well as a precise measurement of time. The signal propagation aspects were particularly demanding, as details relevant to the concept were not available. Further, system engineers were confronted with the design requirements for new receiving and transmitting equipment. Receivers suited for land, sea and air placed further demands. It should be noted that the ongoing war created severe time constraints on expediting the development and later implementation of the system on a nearly global basis.

Background

World War I was primarily fought with weapons and equipment available at its start. Within a year of the start of World War II, demands for new devices, weapons and systems presented broad challenges to the United States scientific and engineering community to meet the needs of England and France as well as the United States.

Response to the challenges sometimes referred to as the physicists' and engineers' war, witnessed a continuing stream of new and frequently complex weapons and systems. It is important to point out that the theoretical information and the technologies available to work with were primitive compared to those at the end of the 20th Century. The technological advances made during the war years probed and pushed the boundaries of science and engineering forward.

The MIT Radiation Laboratory in Cambridge, Massachusetts, was the founding place of Loran. Overall in five years from 1940 to 1945, the broad accomplishments of the Radiation Laboratory, especially in radar (microwaves), have been said to be equal to twenty-five years of progress. Loran, a new and better aid to navigation, using 1950 kHz was unique at the successful Radiation Laboratory devoted primarily to radar.

Not unlike other scientific and engineering developments of the 20th Century, Loran evolved and attained global coverage by the effort and skills of many. Likewise, success of the MIT Radiation Laboratory rests on the talents at the Cambridge site, while industry's role is equally notable.

The story of Loran development and implementation quickly brings to mind Vannevar Bush, James B. Conant, Alfred Loomis, John Alvin Pierce, Richard Woodward, Admiral Julius A. Furer USN, Captain Lawrence M. Harding USCG, Melville Eastham, and others whose contributions to the new systems were substantial.

It should be stressed that beyond the laboratory and industrial production, thousands of civilian and military personnel (heavily USCG) made system implementation possible under the most arduous wartime conditions in impossible geographical locations topped by severe logistic demands. The classification of Loran as "Secret" was a further challenge to be met during the war years. After the war, the classification was removed.

The aforementioned scientists and engineers provide the milestones for the narrative. Considering the events surrounding Loran in the 21st Century loses the anxiety, urgency and importance of the moment in late 1940 when the roots of Loran were formed.

The Setting

On 15 June 1940, the time of the fall of France, President Franklin D. Roosevelt approved the establishment of the National Defense Research Committee (NDRC) under the leadership of Vannevar Bush. Earlier in May, Bush proposed to President Roosevelt the concept of NDRC to coordinate, supervise, and conduct scientific research for war purposes except for flight. The presidential letter appointed the twelve members of the Committee and selected Bush as chairman. The NDRC was established on 27 June 1940 under the National Defense Act of 1916.

Bush, dean of engineering at MIT from 1932-38 and in 1940 President of the Carnegie Institution of Washington, spearheaded all the significant World War II scientific efforts and accomplishments of the war years. His goal was scientific research towards the creation of new military tools and techniques. The NDRC worked in close liaison with the military but independent of its control.

Bush's World War I antisubmarine warfare research experiences in 1917-18 demonstrated to him the need for independence in pursuing scientific and engineering work with the military. This was not lost as he organized the national scientific and engineering resources in 1940 to meet the new German threat. Cooperation between military, scientific and industrial communities does not always prevail.[6]

Alfred L. Loomis

Attention to Alfred L. Loomis, mentioned above, is essential to the Loran narrative. Loomis has sometimes been referred to as "last great amateur of science." His scientific and engineering experience in the period up to World War II included much of the leading technology of the mid-20th

Century. Precise time measurement, microwaves, cyclotron investigation and development, and medical advances were only a part of his experience. In addition, during the 1930s, his personal laboratory that he funded and staffed at Tuxedo Park near New York City included national and international visitors from across the science and engineering spectrum. Microwave studies, later critical to radar, comprised one aspect of the ongoing work at his laboratory.

Loomis was equally at home in the world of academic science at the University of California in Berkeley, California; at MIT at Cambridge, Massachusetts; and on the Washington scene. His achievements on Wall Street in the 1920s provided him with the means to pursue and independently support his scientific interests. In early June 1940, Bush appointed Loomis to be the head of the NDRC Microwave Committee. In the following months, Loomis had full involvement with the Tizard Mission.

The Tizard Mission

Henry Tizard, an English scientist and administrator started in January 1935 with a small committee to address using advances in science and technology to strengthen defense against hostile aircraft. The timely and quick response of his committee brought a December 1935 British government sanction to build the first five radar stations, initially known as Radio Detection Finding (RDF), to detect hostile aircraft. By September 1939, all the radar stations were manned and ready for action.

It became abundantly clear to England, after ten months of war, a newly-surrendered France, and the successful U-boats, that the need for technical superiority plus productive power was essential. England turned toward the United States.

Churchill, becoming Prime Minister in May 1940, supported the concept of a technical exchange with the United States. Most of England's secret war-related technical developments were to be included in the exchange. In August 1940, with the support of Churchill and Roosevelt under Tizard's leadership, the mission (formally called The British Scientific and Engineering Mission to the United States) arrived in Washington to encourage cooperation and share technical knowledge. It was anticipated that even with United States neutrality its industry would develop and produce the British technical secrets.[8]

Detailed sharing of scientific and technical knowledge of wartime developments of weapons and equipments between the two countries had not occurred. The mission's success turned out to be a major event in part because the personnel in Tizard's British mission included a mixed team of scientists and serving officers from Army, Navy and Air Force with battle experience to interface with the United States armed services and others in Washington. The goal of the mission was to provide a basis to develop and build new weapon systems enhanced by the technical exchange. Previously, the neutrality of the United States was a factor that inhibited England's interest in a scientific exchange. British documentation on all the classified wartime developments included books, manuals, circuit diagram, blueprints, films and notes. The 9.5 cm cavity resonant magnetron, developed early in 1940, provided a powerful source of microwaves and became the cornerstone of a number of United States-designed radars in the following five years. This mission and the technical information exchange in the late summer and early fall of 1940 provided the United States with what turned out to be a sixteen-month window of preparation before December 7, 1941.

At the time of the Tizard Mission visit to the United States, it was understood that aircraft bombing of fixed land targets and aircraft hunting enemy submarines needed precise information about their own location. Britain's long range bombing in Europe was constrained because of lack of an aircraft navigation system with a reach into central Europe. It should be noted that in 1937, a British navigation line of sight system providing latitude and longitude was proposed. Location of a ship or aircraft was determined by the time difference of arrival of radio signals (20 to 85 MHz) received from two or more fixed transmitters. Development of the secret system called "Gee" (short for "Grid") began in 1940.

Relevant to this, Tizard put forward his opinion that North America was the ideal place to work on the development of a long-range navigational system because of the on-going hostilities in Britain precluded testing. At that time, the desired system independent of weather conditions should have a range of 1000 miles or greater with an accuracy of the order of 5 miles.[9]

MIT Radiation Laboratory: A Sixteen-Month Head Start

The environment for the exchange was enhanced by the newly formed NDRC under Vannevar Bush with his knowledge and workings of the American scientific academic and industrial community. On October 16, 1940, shortly after the meetings with the Tizard Mission, the NDRC contracted with MIT[*] to be the site for the Radiation Laboratory (Rad Lab) to pursue radar in various forms and to implement the recently- developed British magnetron

---

[*] Loomis, Bush, and other NDRC officials recognized that a civilian research laboratory had to be set up outside of military control, using NDRC funding, to ensure that cavity magnetron technology was developed and deployed as quickly as possible. With Bush and Loomis having strong ties to MIT, it was selected as the location for the new laboratory. The MIT radar research laboratory was originally named the "Microwave Laboratory," but soon became "Radiation Laboratory", or "Rad Lab."

capable of creating powerful microwaves. The first Rad Lab staff meeting was held November 11, and the first assignment on that date was to design and improve night-fighter radar.[10] Officially, the Radiation Lab operated from October 1940 until December 31, 1945.

By March 1941 there were 90 scientists and engineers at work. Late in 1942, the Rad Lab budget reached more than one million dollars; the staff was close to two thousand and in 1945 near four thousand with one-quarter academics and about five hundred of them physicists.11 R&D in Radar was the primary focus of the Rad Lab. All the work at the Rad Lab was at the secret level during the pre-war and war years. This requirement placed another level of difficulty on the efforts.

October 1940-June 1942

Loran Begins

At its meeting on October 1, 1940, the Army Signal Corps Technical Committee established requirements for a "Precision Navigational Equipment for Guiding Airplanes."

In view of the above and recent the consideration of Gee by members of the Tizard group, in October 1940 chairman Loomis of the Microwave Committee proposed, a pulsed hyperbolic ultra high-radio frequency system (30-40 MHz) to meet the Signal Corps requirements. The eventual system at a much lower frequency provided an accuracy of one percent at range of one thousand miles. Research on the systems started immediately by members of the Microwave Committee. In addition to being a strong influence on the Loran group, Loomis provided his personal financing to the early project awaiting government support. In 1959, Loomis was awarded the patent for Loran Long Range Navigation System.

By early spring 1941, the task to investigate this approach was transferred to the MIT Radiation Laboratory with government support. As it was the third Laboratory assigned task, it was referred to as Project III. Initially, the research was identified as LRN for Long Range Navigation (and on occasion Loomis Radio Navigation). The full time navigation group evolved at the Radiation Laboratory under the direction of Melville Eastham, President of the General Radio Company, on leave from Harvard. The starting team of four or five grew to about 30 by 1943.[12]

Initial Loran Efforts

A committee that included members of large electronic companies and the Radiation Laboratory personnel met on December 20, 1940[13] and arranged for the procurement, installation, and field-testing of one pair of transmitting stations and navigation equipment proposed by Loomis.[14] Ranges of 300 to 500 miles for high-flying aircraft were anticipated. At the time of this early procurement, the design and planning included a system operating in the UHF spectrum at frequencies of the order of 30MHz.

First Procurement [15]

Company	Equipment
Bell Laboratories	2 crystal controlled timers
General Electric	1 1.5-megawatt transmitter
RCA	2 receiver-indicators
RCA	6 high frequency pulse triode transmitting tubes
Sperry	2 receiver-indicators (independent design)
Westinghouse	1 2.5-megawatt transmitter

Experimental Phase

Sites for the system's transmitter testing were made available March 24, 1941 when the Radiation Laboratory received permits from the Treasury Department to use two inactive USCG lifeboat stations. One lifeboat station was located at Montauk on Long Island, New York and the other at Fenwick Island, Delaware. These stations provided a 209-mile baseline and were within a reasonable distance of the Bell Telephone Laboratories, the project coordinator. By June 1942, both experimental transmitter sites were operating. These early negotiations eventually in 1942 brought the Coast Guard into the Loran development effort. The Coast Guard's Loran role became important, broad and intensive during the World War II years and beyond.

After system analysis, laboratory and fieldwork, interest in the UHF (30 MHz) part of the radio spectrum waned. One of the system goals was to have navigation coverage of the North Atlantic maritime routes. UHF signal propagation coverage was inadequate. By mid-spring 1941, frequencies of the order of 2000 KHz offered coverage advantages and other attributes.

John Alvin Pierce

Pierce[16] at Harvard Cruft Laboratories from the early 1930's, was experienced in radio propagation, including ionosphere pulse sounding. This aspect of radio wave propagation was critical to the evolving navigation system. On July 1, 1941, at the time when testing of the first hyperbolic radio aid to navigation was about to begin, he took leave from Harvard and worked for nearly five years at the MIT Radiation Laboratory with the navigation system team. His broad and important participation in the Loran development included determining the range of pulsed radio waves when reflected off the lower or E-Layer of the Heaviside layer.[17]

While attending Radiation Laboratory navigation team meetings prior to leaving Harvard, Pierce designed and had constructed a pair of 5 kW 2000 kHz pulse transmitters. The lower frequency transmitters were installed for testing at the Delaware and Long Island former USCG stations.

Propagation tests were made between September 3 and 22, 1941. The main receiving station was set up in the Ann Arbor, Michigan home of a University of Michigan professor. Pierce installed receiving equipment in a station wagon and made signal measurements at Springfield, Missouri and Frankfort, Kentucky. The tests indicated the possibility of stable sky-wave transmission. A range of 1000 miles with the low power transmitters and the ground wave range proved greater than expected. As a result, the work at UHF was abandoned before the delivery of much of the equipment on order.[18]

Pierce emphasized in his report of the measurement trip the need for an improved method for reading time difference. During the next several months, efforts by the Radiation Laboratory navigation team developed a trace cathode ray tube indicator capable of a 1microsecond measurement and a multiple trace for pulse matching the signal from the master and slave stations. Direct synchronization at lower frequencies was also achieved.

A month after Pearl Harbor, Pierce made additional 2.8 MHz-8.5 MHz long-range signal measurements in Bermuda. Satisfactory ground waves from the 5 KW transmitters were measured at a range of about 720 miles. Importantly, these tests established the practicability of nighttime sky waves from the E layer of the ionosphere. After further enhancement to transmitter performance, 1950 KHz was adopted as the frequency of interest.[19]

Admiral Julius A. Furer

At the outbreak of World War II, Admiral Furer became the Coordinator of the Research and Development and the senior member of the NDRC. He coordinated widespread research that sped development of modern weapons systems for the Navy. These services won Furer the Legion of Merit on 30 June 1945. Based on the results of the navigation system testing, Furer felt that a navigational aid might be developed.[20] His support, together with that of others, helped to bring about this practical long-range navigation system to aid in the war effort.

In late March 1942, signal test results at 2000 kHz showing significant ground wave coverage and improved cathode ray tube presentation of the signals led Melville Eastham to present the results of this ongoing laboratory and fieldwork to representatives of the Joint Chiefs of Staff. He also proposed a series of tests along the Atlantic seaboard to determine maximum range and the possible development of an aid to navigation.

The plan was to construct a chain of stations installed and operated by NDRC. with results to be submitted to those were most interested. The Army showed little or no interest, and Admiral Furer suggested that the Radiation Laboratory carry out the plan and keep him apprised.[21] The test sites would be located along the United States and Canadian Atlantic coasts. In the middle of May 1942, Canada agreed to cooperate and with two sites in Nova Scotia complementing the two United States sites. This was a beginning.

Admiral Furer, observing the evolving long range navigation system, felt that Navy guidance and assistance should be available to the ongoing research at the Radiation Laboratory. Further, an emerging aid to navigation system in the future would come under the USCG. In keeping with this and mindful of the Coast Guard ongoing responsibility for United States Aids to Navigation, with support from Captain F. R. Furth of the office of VCNO, Captain Lawrence M. Harding USCG was assigned as Navy liaison officer in the development and implementation of the navigation system. He was assigned as naval representative for Loran to the Radiation Laboratory and to undertake any necessary field activities.

Captain Harding, formerly of the U.S. Lighthouse Service, was deeply experienced in marine radio beacon technology. The future jurisdiction and administration of Loran by the USCG stemmed from this early and increasing wartime involvement with the evolving navigation system. Intensive and broad participation characterizes the role of the USCG through the WWII years and beyond. Because of Loran's utmost secrecy, Harding's orders to temporary duty at Cambridge, Massachusetts were unknown to his immediate supervisors. It is interesting that Harding became responsible for the system designation acronym "Loran" (Long Range Navigation).

System Test

With the 100 kW transmitters installed and tested in June 1942, it was important to determine as quickly as possible whether Loran had practical and immediate value to the war effort; Harding initiated a month long sea test on the Coast Guard weather ship *USS Manasquan* to determine the service range of the system. Observations and tests were also to be conducted on board a Navy blimp by Pierce. Military aircraft flights equipped with Loran to determine performance and range were scheduled.

Blimp K-2 Test

The first demonstration of the use of Loran was made using transmissions from the Fenwick, Delaware and the Montauk, New York experimental stations, Pierce made readings during the K-2 blimp test, on June 13, 1942. Pierce's measurements were made on an improved model of the laboratory receiver-indicator as the airship transited 250 miles between Lakehurst, New Jersey and Ocean City, Maryland and passed over lighthouses, bridges, and towers with accurate map locations. Loran charts were not available and readings were recorded as the various identifiable points were passed. Calculations the following week indicated errors of less than 20 yards, and the average of all errors was zero, to the nearest microsecond.[22]

With the airship ready to return from Maryland, Pierce decided to home along a line of position from a distance of 50 to 75 miles offshore. With the Loran receiver turned off for an hour and the airship somewhere over the Atlantic Ocean, the receiver was turned on and set for the known reading at Lakehurst. Adjustments were made to the flight course in accordance with the Loran readings to head for the hangar. Upon landing, the blimp headed for the exact *middle* of the hangar.

USS Manasquan Test

Likewise, the month-long sea test June 17 to July 17, 1942 aboard *USS Manasquan* confirmed estimated values for sky wave performance at night and determined the range of service as 1400 nautical miles at night 700 for ground waves in the daytime. It was observed that in inclement weather not suitable for celestial navigation, that Loran provided the capability to maintain a useful line of position from one pair of stations.

Airborne Tests

On July 4, 1942 a B-24 equipped with a Loran laboratory receiver indicator made a test flight from Boston to Cape Sable, Nova Scotia. System performance data was obtained with signals from the Fenwick, Delaware and Montauk, New York transmitters.

On November 1, 1942, a PBY flight to Bermuda demonstrated the use of Loran in obtaining fixes. The results from these tests provided a basis for system expansion and its recommendation to navigational agencies.[23]

Summary: Mid-1942

The complete receiver design was completed and an order for 250 Loran receivers for ships was place with the Fada Radio & Electric Company. Philco was the builder of Loran receivers for aircraft. Loran transmitters with 100 KW, operating at 1950 KHz, provided ground-wave range of about 600 to 700 nautical miles over sea water and sky-wave range out to 1300 to 1400 nautical miles by night. Position errors were estimated at about one percent of the distance from the Loran transmitting station.

System Expansion Begins

The above mentioned June and July systems tests, notably the blimp test, resulted in immediate high level interest in the navigation system. The Navy, Army, and NDRC took steps to apply the system to the war effort. The Navy requested NDRC to immediately procure equipment and install Loran stations in Newfoundland, Labrador, and Greenland. Receivers were to be acquired for key United States and Canadian vessels.[24]

Responsibility was given to the Army Signal Corps to procure airborne receivers for all services. Additional Northeastern Atlantic installations as well as the in the Aleutian region were planned. The Navy Bureau of Ships and the Coast Guard were assigned full responsibility covering all aspects of the system, including the training of operators and technicians for ground and shipboard equipment

Following arrangements with the Canadian government, a slave station constructed at Baccaro, Nova Scotia operated with the double-pulsed master at Montauk Point and at a different pulse rate with a second master station constructed at Deming, Nova Scotia. By October 1, 1942, the stations went into operation under the Royal Canadian Navy. These stations were the beginning of providing the Loran navigation system coverage across the Atlantic to the European Theater of war. Navigation assistance was essential for the wartime convoys. The two Canadian stations and Fenwick and Montauk provided operations 16 hours per day with the stations manned by US Coast Guard and Canadian Navy personnel standing watches supervised by NDRC engineers.[25]

On January 1, 1943, authority over Loran was transferred from the NDRC MIT Radiation Laboratory to the Navy. On the same day, the Coast Guard assumed operation of the Montauk and Fenwick stations. At the same time, the Navy Hydrographic Office assumed responsibility for the computation, drafting, reproduction, and distribution of the Loran charts and tables. Radiation Laboratory prepared the early charts. For the Radiation Laboratory Loran team and the US Coast Guard, the North Atlantic, Aleutian, and Pacific Loran chains were in the future.

Endnotes

[1] James Phinney Baxter 3rd, *Scientists Against Time*, MIT Press, Cambridge, MA, 1968, p. 151.

[2] Henry E Guerlac, *Radar in WW II*, American Institute of Physics, Tomash, New York, NY, 1987, p. 531.

[3] Baxter, *op. cit.,* p. 142.

[4] Robert Buderi, *The Invention that Changed the World*, Simon and Schuster, New York, NY, 1996, p. 252.

[5] Malcolm F. Willoughby, *U.S. Coast Guard in World War II,* USNI, Annapolis, MD, 1987p.150.

[6] Jennet Conant, *Tuxedo Park,* Simon & Schuster, New York, NY, 2002, p. 163-64.

[7] C. P. Cnow, *Science and Government,* Mentor Book, New York, NY, p. 37.

[8] Buderi, *op. cit.,* p. 31.

[9] Conant, *op. cit.,* p. 181, 198, 231.

[10] Orrin E. Dunlap, Jr. *Radar,* Harper & Brothers, New York, NY, 1946, p. 132.

[11] Daniel Kevles, *The Physicists,* Alfred A. Knopf, New York, Y, 1978, p 107.

[12] John A. Pierce, editor, *Loran: Volume 4 MIT Radiation Laboratory Series*, 1948, p.21.

[13] *ibid.,* p. 21

[14] The Coast Guard at War: IV Loran, Volume 1, Section 1, Chapter 1, p. 5. http:www.uscg.mil/hq/g-cp/history/Loran_1.html

[15] Pierce, *op. cit.,* p.20.

[16] John A. Pierce received 1990 IEEE Medal for Engineering Excellence "For the design, teaching, and advocacy of radio propagation, navigation and timing which led to Loran, Loran C, and Omega."

[17] John A. Pierce, Memoirs of John Alvin Pierce: Development of Loran, Navigation: *Journal of the Institute of Navigation,* Vol. 36, No. 1, Spring 1989, p. 4.

[18] Guerlac, *op. cit.,* p. 526.

[19] Guerlac, *op, cit.,* p. 528.

[20] Wiiloughby, *op. cit.,* p. 152.

[21] The Coast Guard at War: IV Loran, Volume 1, Section 1, Chapter 1, p. 6. http:www.uscg.mil/hq/g-cp/history/Loran_1.html

[22] John A. Pierce, Memoirs of John Alvin Pierce: Development of Loran, Navigation: *Journal of the Institute of navigation,* Vol. 36, No. 1, Spring 1989, p. 5.

[23] John A. Pierce, editor, *Loran: Volume 4 MIT Radiation Laboratory Series*, 1948, p. 404.

[24] Guerlac, *op. cit.,* p. 529.

[25] Guerlac, *op. cit.,* p. 530.

Cold War Physicist: Nicholas Christofilos

Introduction[*]

Nicholas Christofilos was born in 1916 near Fenway Park in Boston. When he was seven, his parents returned to Athens, Greece, where his father, who had been proprietor of the Wellington Café in Boston, resumed ownership of a coffee house. Christofilos retained his American citizenship and returned to the United States in 1953, engaging in scientific pursuits until his untimely death in 1972.[1] In his nineteen years of participation in the United States at the cutting edge of science, he made a difference. Held in high regard, he was an international figure in the scientific world.

Two of his most imaginative defense projects known to the public are Project Argus and Project Sanguine. Project Argus in 1958, cited as the "world's largest scientific experiment," was proposed in 1957 by Christofilos while working at the Lawrence Radiation Laboratory of the University of California.[2] This successful geophysical experiment was conducted by the Navy under the supervision of the Defense Department and the Atomic Energy Commission in August and September of the following year. The global scale endeavor involved civilian scientists from government, academia, and industry and participation from other branches of the United States Armed Forces.

In the summer of 1958, Christofilos attended a briefing by the Polaris Special Projects Office and became aware of broad, difficult, and unresolved Navy requirements to communicate from the continental United States to a deeply submerged Polaris submarine. He proposed using

---

[*] From 1962-1972, the author had occasion to be involved with Nicholas Christofilos in regard to the evolving Navy ELF global submarine radio communication system.

electromagnetic waves in the Extremely Low Frequency (ELF) range of 10-100 Hz. The proposal provided the impetus for the initial research phase of the communication system development known as Sanguine, which later evolved into a Navy operational system in 1987. The system fulfilled certain needs of United States strategic and tactical submarines, primarily to send secure communications to a submarine at operating depth anywhere in the world.

Christofilos, considered the father of ELF communications, remained a strong advocate and partisan during the long system development until his premature death in 1972. Widely remembered by his Navy and industry associates on the ELF team, a modest memorial was established in his name with Sigma Xi. All of his scientific endeavors were large scale, on the cutting edge of science, and significant. Further, in general his work was classified. Today, some still remain so.

The January 1973 issue of <u>Physics Today</u> noted, "Christofilos was intensely proud of his American birth and citizenship. He understood well the military needs of the Nation and conscientiously devoted a significant fraction of his life to improving the US strategic posture." It seems that from the time Christofilos returned to the United States, his center of attention was science frequently with a direct or nuanced military attribute. At the time of his passing, the <u>New York Times</u> identified him as "foremost nuclear physicist." His participation in addressing solutions to military needs during the Cold War era warrants attention to his efforts.

About Christofilos

Current media provided a variety of ways to cite his talents: "One of the most original thinkers in physics of his generation", "An unconventional Greek Scientist named

Nicholas Christofilos", "The right kind of nuclear detonation would threaten hundreds of satellites. That is because of something called the "Christofilos Effect", "Nicholas Christofilos suggested that a portion of the earth's interior could be used as a launching pad to propagate ELF signals", "Nicholas C. Christofilos is the lone-wolf genius behind Project Argus, a global experiment that has been called 'the most grandiose single scientific venture in history'", and "A Plasma Physics Pioneer".

1923-1952

A boy of 7 when he went to Athens, in these years Christofilos witnessed the post World War I scene and in 1936 the establishment of a dictatorship followed by German occupation troops (1941-1945), and civil war (1946-1949). As a young person, in addition to an interest in building radio equipment, he displayed considerable talent as a promising musician. It is notable that when the German occupation of Greece ended in 1945, Christofilos composed the music for the celebration marking the end.

Graduating in 1938, from the National Technical University in Athens, with advanced degrees in electrical and mechanical engineering from the National Technical University in Athens, he worked for Wisk, Inc., an Athens company installing and maintaining elevators in apartments and office buildings. In 1941, the Germany army of occupation directed the company to repair trucks for the military. Christofilos was assigned as supervisor of a truck repair terminal. At the end of World War II, he established his own elevator installation business.[3]

Throughout the German occupation, demands on Christofilos's time were decreased. At that point, he had no formal physics credentials. During this time and essentially alone, he began his private and continuing study of atomic physics. German textbooks were available in Greek bookstores, and his readings covered nuclear reactions, isotopes, and high voltages. The work of the Kaiser Wilhelm Institute in Berlin, where nuclear fission had been discovered in 1938, was of particularly interested him. This direction pointed to particle acceleration to relativistic speeds using his novel concept of the strong-focusing principle of magnetic containment for particle accelerators. In 1946, and with more detail in 1947, he applied for Greek and American patents for a particle accelerator of his own design.[4]

On several occasions, during the later 1940s, Christofilos sent letters of his designs to the Radiation Laboratory at the University of California in Berkeley. The scientists here decided that the mathematics was not clear and the patent proposals were filed and half forgotten.

Christofilos continued to work on his design of accelerators to speed nuclear particles to significantly high energy levels. Then current accelerator technology used very large magnets. To achieve efficiency in the accelerator construction and to achieve very high energy levels, he developed the concept of strong focusing reducing the need for large magnets and providing higher energy levels to the particles. A further patent application on March 10, 1950, proposed a particle accelerator with strong focusing providing energy a magnitude higher than that obtained with much larger and more expensive "weak" focusing magnets. The United States "strong focusing" patent 2,736,799 was awarded to Christofilos February 28, 1956.[5]

In the December 1952 *Physical Review*, several members of the Brookhaven National Laboratory proposed a strong-focusing accelerator. The scientists were unaware of the earlier work by Christofilos in developing a similar strong-focusing technique. Later, these scientists publicly acknowledged Christofilos in the July 1953 issue of the *Physical Review*. "Since Christophilos's manuscript is known to have been prepared in early 1950, it is obvious that his proposal antedates ours by over two years. We are, therefore happy to acknowledge his priority."

In "A Tribute to Nicholas C. Christofilos," T. K. Fowler of the Lawrence Livermore Laboratory noted, "His early contribution to this mainstay of the accelerator art of today was all the more remarkable in that he conceived and worked out these ideas while in almost complete isolation from any modern, active, scientific community."[6]

During the following years, strong focusing was successfully used in accelerators at Cornell, Harvard, MIT, Daresbury, Hamburg and Yerevan; and in proton accelerators at Brookhaven, CERN, Serpukhov and the National Accelerator Laboratory. As mentioned above, Christofilos in 1946 also independently invented an accelerator similar to the synchrotron. In 1963, the Franklin Institute awarded Christofilos for the synchrotron,[7] contributions to high-energy beams, and other achievements. Recognition and wide application of his inventiveness came after his return to the United States.

As the 1940s closed, Christofilos was unknown in the United States. His credit as an elevator engineer eclipsed his unlettered abilities as an atomic physicist. He continued to write letters suggesting ways to build an improved accelerator. The scientists at the Berkeley Radiation Laboratory still found Christofilos's mathematics crude and in replying pointed out his errors.

Later in 1952, upon reexamination of his latest letter there was agreement by the Berkeley Radiation Laboratory scientists that the Christofilos design was a major contribution to high-energy physics. Further, there was also favorable interest in Christofilos at the Brookhaven, Long Island, New York, National Laboratory, then involved with the design and construction of an accelerator

1953

In February 1953, Christofilos returned to the United States to meet with members of the Atomic Energy Commission (AEC) and to press for consideration of his accelerator design. After meetings with AEC patent officers, in return for a $10,000 payment, a license and agreement were granted for use by the United States government and its contractors of the Christofilos "strong focusing" principle.[8]

The Brookhaven Laboratory was so impressed that he was immediately hired to work on the $29 million accelerator, based on his design and under construction there.[9]   The Brookhaven Alternating Gradient Synchrotron, a proton accelerator, was the first application of Christofilos's strong focusing. Overall, the principles of the strong focusing techniques brought government savings of $70 million.

Astron

During December 1951, in addition to the government weapons laboratory at Los Alamos, a second weapons laboratory known as University of California Radiation Laboratory, Livermore (UCRL), was started. Research and development at the new laboratory were directed to the investigation of thermonuclear techniques for weapons and other purposes. By 1956, the laboratory was heavily involved in thermonuclear research. The Army and Navy patronized Los Alamos for their weapons while the Air Force was oriented toward Livermore.

While at Brookhaven in the mid-1950s, Christofilos's thinking returned to the concept of controlled fusion, at the time highly classified. His interest in fusion had begun eight years before when he was still in Greece. His idea was considered one of the biggest problems in applied physics:

how to use magnetic fields to contain high-energy plasmas and produce a controlled thermonuclear reaction. The purpose was to provide unlimited electric power from controlled thermonuclear reactions. He filed for a patent for a device to achieve this by magnetic trapping of plasma to release fusion energy.[10]

Christofilos obtained a position at the Livermore Laboratory, directing the program to produce a controlled thermonuclear reaction called Astron, supported by the AEC and the Department of Defense. Astron-related research began at UCRL in 1956.

"In November 1964, Christofilos and two colleagues reported to the American Physical Society that they had observed trapping of the electrons in the Astron. The effect lasted for a thousandth of a second at a temperature of nearly 200,000,000 degrees."[11]

It has been noted that the Defense Department's interest "was no doubt related to its long-term concern with the practicality of using intense particle beams for military purposes. In fact, the electron accelerator designed by Christofilos has played a major role in the free-electron laser program at the Lawrence Livermore Laboratory, an important component of the Reagan administration's Strategic Defense Initiative."[12] In the following years, in addition to the Astron involvement, he continued to make important contributions to the accelerator field in the development of proton linear accelerations and collective accelerators.[13]

Project Argus

Artificial Radiation Belts

Shortly after the October 5, 1957 successful launch of the satellite Sputnik on October 5, 1957 Christofilos looked into creating an artificial radiation belt in the upper region of the earth's atmosphere with a nuclear detonation at a high altitude, about 300 miles from the surface of the earth. The earth's magnetic field would be used to trap electrons released by the atomic detonations. These considerations were concurrent with the ongoing International Geophysical Year (IGY), July 1 1957 to December 31, 1958,

In January 1958, UCRL published Christofilos's proposal, classified because of its military applications, to use the earth's magnetic field to trap electrons injected at the proper altitude (about 300 miles from the surface of the earth) from detonated small atomic bombs. The very extensive experiment that followed to validate Christophilos's prediction of results took place in late August and September of 1958 and was called Project Argus.

Christofilos postulated that electrons from the atomic bombs trapped in the magnetic field would provide an artificial radiation belt. Understanding would be gained regarding the impact of the trapped particles in various areas of scientific interest including radio communications, space flight, and knowledge regarding the magnetic and radiation environment in the near-earth space. Christofilos's prediction about particle entrapment, proven by Project Argus, is now referred to as the *Christofilos Effect*.

The military importance of Christofilos's classified paper caught the attention of the Chairman of the President's Science Advisory Committee (PSAC). Under the aegis of PSAC, a February 1958 scientific working group convened for several weeks at the University of California Radiation Laboratory to assess the theory and its potential military applications.

Later, a presentation regarding whether the Project Argus trapping experiment should be undertaken was made to President Eisenhower's PSAC. Support for the Project was encouraged by Van Allen's recent discovery of the radiation belt of the earth. Christofilos vigorously discussed his theories about the *"Christofilos Effect"* to the Committee. On May 1, 1958 the PSAC recommendation to undertake Argus was made to the President who concurred.

Within four months, Project Argus experiments took place involving the space encircling the entire earth. The operational and technological management of the project was the responsibility of the then new DOD Advanced Research Projects Agency (ARPA). As mentioned above the Navy directed the experiment with participation by other branches of the Armed Forces. The goal of Argus was to examine the physics of the results from the three high-altitude nuclear bursts called Argus I, II, and III. The satellite *Explorer IV* was launched successfully on July 26, 1958. Operating as planned, it provided the principal body of observations of the artificial radiation belts. Analysis of *Explorer IV* data on the natural radiation belt as well as on the artificial radiation belts from the Argus bursts propelled the entire subject to a new level of understanding and broad scientific interest.

Prior to the Argus tests that took place in late August and September, in March 1958 (as part of the IGY) earth-circling Satellite Explorer I, recently launched, monitored the detonations of atomic weapons in space over Johnston Island in the Pacific. Examination of the data from the Geiger counter on the satellite led to the discovery of the radiation belt of the earth a massive region of space populated by energetic charged particles (principally electrons and protons), trapped within the external geomagnetic field.[*] The radiation belt was named The Van Allen Belt to honor one of the Argus Project's participating and contributing physicists James A. Van Allen. Later in a 1960 lecture at Ohio State University, Van Allen referring to Argus said it was "one of the greatest experiments in pure science ever conducted."

Navy Project Argus Task Force

Tarawa	aircraft carrier
Norton Sound	missile-testing ship
Albemarle	seaplane tender
Bearss	destroyer
Warrington	destroyer
Courtney	destroyer escort
Hammerberg	destroyer escort
Nesho	oiler
Salamonie	oiler destroyer escort

Tests

"Task Force 88," a fleet of nine US Navy vessels including the USS *Norton Sound,* Navy's floating missile launch pad, provided the support for warhead shots. The three tests made from this experimental guided missile ship were on August 27 and 30 and September 6 from a location in the South Atlantic east of Patagonia and south of the Falkland Islands about 1100 miles southwest of Cape Town, South Africa. The 1.7-kiloton atomic warheads were detonated at altitudes of 100, 182 and 466 miles.[14]

A modified version of the Polaris re-entry test vehicle (RTV-30) launched the bombs from the deck of the *USS*

---

[*]http://www.aip.org/history/ead/iowa_java_papers/19990077_content.ht ml

Norton Sound. The vehicle was a set of solid-fueled rockets used to try out components for the missile that the Navy was developing for launching from submerged submarines. The entire assembly was about fifty-seven feet tall. All three shots were successfully launched from a pitching ship in an open ocean.[15]

The atomic explosions sent electrons racing back and forth along the magnetic meridians extending about 4000 miles into space. Electrons created man-made aurora when they hit the atmosphere. Traveling with the speed of light, the band of electrons enveloped the earth in an hour and provided a man-made shell of radiation in August and September 1958.

Satellite *Explorer IV,* equipped with Geiger counters and successfully launched on 26 July 1958, provided the principal body of observations of the artificial radiation belts and natural radiation belt. Additionally, rockets sent up from the United States and other locations provided data. Worldwide conditions created by the detonations were monitored around the world in conjunction with the Geophysical Year activities.

Monitoring took various forms. For example, the Army's Signal Research and Development Laboratory installed two huge loops designed to observe magnetic waves on frequencies as low as one cycle per second. A loop in a remote location south of the Grand Canyon enclosed twenty-six square miles. Two similar loops with effective areas of twelve and twenty-three square miles were place in operation in Burlington County, New Jersey and recorded the pulses from the explosions until the completion of the Argus experiment.[16]

The results of the tests supported Christofilos' predictions. The project was accomplished under careful secrecy and it was not until March 1959 that the media including Business Week, Life, Newsweek, and Time weekly magazines,[17] and importantly the New York Times provided news of the Argus experiment in sufficient detail for the public to grasp the scale and some aspects of the importance of the effort. The *Christofilos Effect* was proven and established.

A later assessment of Argus concluded that the purpose appeared to be to assess the impact of high altitude nuclear explosions on radio transmission and radar operations because of the electro-magnet pulse (EMP) and an understanding of the geomagnetic field and the behavior of the charge particles in it.

Requirements[18] Polaris Strategic Submarine Radio Communication

The Problem

The Navy needed a communication system to transmit command and control messages to new Fleet Ballistic Missile (FBM) strategic submarines operating in a stealth mode globally. Initial research started in 1958; for the next four years, the Navy sponsored a wide range of exploratory technical efforts towards a solution for the strategic submarine communication need.

At this stage in the Cold War and until the 1970s, the concept for this communication system included the additional requirement for ability to withstand a nuclear attack at the transmission site. It was intended that the system be able to send Emergency Action Messages (EAM) after absorbing a substantial nuclear attack. The impact of nuclear bursts over the transmission path also received attention. These needs plus global coverage, a continental United States transmitter location and the other unique requirements presented a daunting task. For more than ten years, additional challenges to the researchers arose from the secret classification of all aspects of the work.

A brief review of the requirements brings out the extent of the challenge. The technology available then compared to current capability appears primitive. This is especially true regarding computer technology. Cold war expediency and secrecy were further obstacles. A radio communication system to match the remarkable stealth capability needs of the new strategic Polaris submarine was not at hand.

FBM Submarine
Communication Requirements (circa 1957)

Error-free one-way communication
Hard copy in a specified time
Transmitter in Continental U.S (CONUS)
No severe reduction in speed, maneuverability, or
depth of the submarine
Coverage of the submarine's operating areas
Resistance to jamming
Transmitter to withstand nuclear attack

Christofilos Recommends

In the summer of 1958 at the time of the Argus experiment, Christofilos, a member of the Polaris Command Communications Committee (PCCC) attended a briefing by the Polaris Special Projects Office. There, he became aware of Navy's requirement to communicate from CONUS to a deeply submerged submarine. In August, he proposed a communication system to use electromagnetic waves in the range 10-100 Hz. Christofilos's early classical music training in Greece provided the metaphoric title for his proposal called "Clarinet Bassoon" (a low note).

In this first approach, the idea was to resonate the earth-ionosphere cavity at its natural modes. The Navy gave immediate attention to the Bassoon concept. The Navy pursued ELF (3-300 Hz) for the submarine communication system. Christofilos, considered the father of ELF communications, remained a strong advocate and partisan during the long system development until his premature death in 1972. His membership in the PCCC brought Christofilos into contact with senior personnel from a variety of academic, industrial, Navy, and government organizations. The Committee met on a frequent basis and was apprised of the status of the evolving ELF system.

The Navy immediately took an intense interest in ELF transmission because of the following characteristics of such a system:

> Low signal attenuation in sea water
> Low signal propagation attenuation
> Comparatively low sensitivity at ELF to atmospheric
> disturbances caused by nuclear blasts in the signal path
> Better survivability against nuclear attack (ELF transmitters
> and antenna arrays lend themselves to dispersion and hardening)

Early ELF R&D

Similar to all of Christofilos's interests ELF was also global in concept and on a scale of unusual magnitude. For example the first experimental transmitting antenna that was constructed in 1962 to perform ELF signal propagation measurements on land and on submarines was 110 miles long and reached from North Carolina to Virginia. Using ELF for global communications was unique. This brought with it the need to understand electromagnetic noise on a worldwide basis. Selecting a suitable location for a United States based transmitter required knowledge of the earth conductivity in many of the states. The challenges to creating and building a system were innumerable.

211

ELF Test 1963

In early 1963, January to April, the Navy conducted an extensive communication demonstration between a shore-based ELF (30-300 Hz) transmitter located in North Carolina and the nuclear submarine *USS Seawolf* (SSN-575) operating in the North Atlantic at a range of 2400 miles with its receiving antenna near keel depth. Signals were received at a range of 535 miles with the antenna at greater depths. During these weeks of communication tests, in addition to the submarine, fixed land, and mobile van measurements signal propagation measurements were made. Atmospheric noise measurements were made in the United States, South America, and on Malta.

By June 1963, data from the submarine and land-based propagation and atmospheric noise measurements were analyzed. As a result, ELF became a candidate for a system to communicate to the Polaris submarines operating deep in global locations. Many important and detailed questions remained to be resolved by theoretical, laboratory and field efforts.

ELF System Completed

After decades of advances in the technology applicable to the transmitting and receiving needs of an ELF system, solutions were found for a wide range of problems (technical, non-technical, fiscal, political, and environment-related) and the system was completed. Transmitters and antennas were constructed in Wisconsin and Michigan, submarines were equipped, operational use established and personnel trained. This initiative by President Reagan early in his first administration provided the driving force that culminated in the operational transfer of ELF in October 1989 to Operation Commander, Naval Telecommunications

Command, from the Space and Naval Warfare Systems Command.

When the strategic and attack submarine communication system became operational, it provided reception by the submarine at depth and speed. The ultimate ELF system was different from the early concepts. As previously mentioned, the system and its performance were considerably enhanced by the advent of the steadily improving computer capability as well as the creativity of the various laboratories involved. Except for the choice of operating frequencies, the Navy's operating ELF system was far removed from the early 1960s concept. Initially the system was designed for the FBM submarine. By the mid-1970s, based on data and experience from many tests aboard the strategic and attack submarines, a tactical and strategic operational concept matured.

Christofilos innovated; but the work to create a system to meet the basic requirements was a significant challenge and involved a great number of industrial, government, and academic organizations over a period of many years. ELF coming on line operationally took place almost thirty years after Nicholas Christofilos's suggestion that ELF should be considered as a candidate for radio communication to submarines at depth and speed. The system as built was not one that Christofilos envisioned but it did operate at ELF as he originally suggested.

2004

At the end of September 2004, after fifteen years of communication with strategic and tactical submarines, the ELF system was closed down and dismantled.

Conclusion

Particle accelerators, Astron, Project Argus and the Navy's ELF program are not disparate. All have their roots in magnetic and electric fields. Further, each originated by Christofilos. Each also required unbridled thought and were on a scale that is always large and in some instances global. Perhaps the word <u>unique</u> would be appropriate for each of the three concepts. Certainly, Nicholas Christofilos was himself unique.

As a citizen, Christofilos returned to the United States in 1953. For the following nineteen years, his contributions to science and the nation's strategic posture were significant. His efforts bracketed most of the Cold War era.

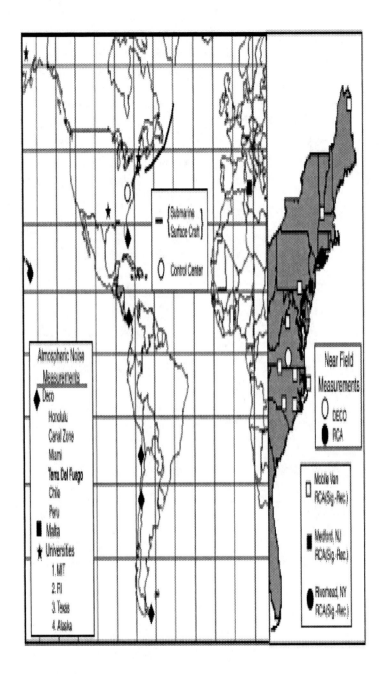

Experimental ELF
Intensive Test January-April 1963

WISCONSIN/MICHIGAN ELF TRANSMITTERS

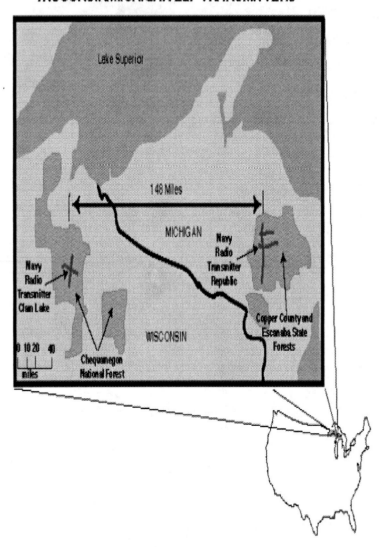

Endnotes

[1] I last conversed by phone with Nick at the Livermore Laboratory regarding a technical matter two days prior to his passing.

[2] John S. Foster, T. Kenneth Fowler, and Frederick E. Mills, "Nicholas C. Christofilos 1916-1972," *Physics Today*, 26(1) (1973) p.109-115.

[3] Current Biography 1965, The HW Wilson Company, Bronx, New York, p. 82-84.

[4] Dictionary of Scientific Biography, Charles Scribner's Sons, New York, 1970, p. 166.

[5] *Ibid*; p. 166.

[6] "A Tribute to Nicholas C. Christofilos," by T. K. Fowler, Associate Director, Controlled Thermonuclear Research Lawrence Livermore Laboratory Livermore, California http://accelconf.web.cern.ch/AccelConf/p73/PDF/PAC1973_0035.PDF - 114.8KB.

[7] Foster et al, *op. cit.,* p. 109-115.

[8] Dictionary of Scientific Biography, *op. cit.,* p. 167.

[9] New York Times, March 19, 1979, p. 16.

[10] http://www-istp.gsfc.nasa.gov/Education/whtrap1.html p.2.

[11] Current Biography 1965, *op. cit.,* p. 84.

[12] Dictionary of Scientific Biography, *op. cit.,* p. 167.

[13] "A Tribute to Nicholas C. Christofilos," by T. K. Fowler, Associate Director, Controlled Thermonuclear Research Lawrence Livermore Laboratory Livermore, California http://accelconf.web.cern.ch/AccelConf/p73/PDF/PAC1973_0035.PDF - 114.8KB..

[14] http://nuclearweaponarchive.org/Usa/Tests/Argus.html

[15] Walter Sullivan, *Assault on the Unknown: The International Geophysical Year,* McGraw-Hill Book Company, Inc., New York, 1961, p. 152

[16] *Ibid,* p. 159

[17] Business Week, 28 March 1959, p. 32-33, Life, 30 March 1959, p. 31-34, Newsweek, 30 March 1959, p. 58-59, Time, 30 March 1959, 70-71, 16 November 1959, p. 100.

[18] John Merrill, *A History of Extremely Low Frequency (ELF) Submarine Radio Communications,* Publishing Directions, LLC, 615 Queen St., Southington, CT 06489, 2002. This version of the forty years of ELF history was written in response to a discussion in a 1993 meeting of the ELF Environmental Review Committee held in Sault Ste. Marie, Michigan. At that meeting and subsequent meetings, it was concluded that a history of the ELF system and its development was lacking. In 1999, the author was invited to write the history.

U.S. Navy and 20th Century Oceanography:

Summary 1900-1960

Part I

> "This new big science is called oceanography. It is the whole business of getting into the sea, finding out what is there, what is underneath, studying its chemistry, its physics…"[1]
>
> (Circa 1972)

Environment

Oceans with an average depth of 13,000 feet comprise about seventy-one percent of the total area of the earth and this provides an enormous challenge for ships on the surface and submarines below. Naval operational success at sea is dependent on knowledge concerning the sea's natural and man-made ambient noise, current, tides, turbulence, depths, temperature, salinity, underwater ridges, winds, ice, and internal waves. Today, precise details and understanding of the sea is required for successful strategic and tactical operations with modern naval technology. At the start of the 20th century knowledge of the sea was at best fragmentary.

Although oceanography began when some first fact about the sea was observed and recorded, "…it was not until about the middle of the nineteenth century that systematic examination even of the surface of the sea was seriously undertaken, or that scientists awoke to the fact that the underlying waters offered a whole new world of exploration."[2] Twentieth century technology advancements aided the broadening of marine research about the physical, chemical, and geological aspects of the seas. This new knowledge addressed Navy needs.

Throughout the entire 20th century that included two world wars, almost continuous improvements and advances in military technology; ships, aircraft, submarines, and weapons brought new challenges. The Navy required a more complete knowledge of the oceans to address at-sea operational requirements.

An effective relationship gradually developed between the Navy and the growing marine science community each with divergent needs, one with science as the goal and the other with at-sea operational requirements. The Navy needed knowledge of the sea.

Preface

In April 1900, John Holland delivered *Holland VI*, his modest but practical submarine, to the United States Navy. By the start of World War I (WWI), there were about 400 submarines worldwide. During the entire 20th century, along with the universal acceptance of the submarine there was an increasing demand for detailed knowledge of the nature of the submarine's operational environment, the sea. Detecting and evading submarines became an imperative of the 20th century.

In 1973, an oceanographer assessing support for marine science in the United States for the period 1850-1940 concluded, "For marine science, a half-century of active if not sympathetic government support was over. In the next 40 years, those before the beginning of World War II (WWII), oceanography in the United States was largely supported by private institutions."[3]

WWII and the remainder of the 20th century witnessed a significant increase in Navy joint ventures with private sector marine science laboratories. An article in the November 1980 issue of <u>Fortune</u> noted that oceanography, an expensive science, was receiving a good portion of naval funds available for research on that science.[4]

Roots for government support of gathering and disseminating ocean information became more highly focused in 1866, when an Act of Congress established the Hydrographic Office. The Act expanded hydrographic work and included "the carrying out of surveys, the collection of information and the printing of every kind of nautical chart or publication." The Hydrographic Office provided oceanic support for the Navy by focusing on physical conditions, boundaries and currents; oceanography in addition includes study of marine life, physical chemistry of the ocean, and the geology of the ocean bottom. In 1962, the Hydrographic Office was designated the U.S. Naval Oceanographic Office.

The U.S. Coast and Geodetic Survey (C&GS) authorized in 1878 under the Treasury Department provided scientific support for marine research. In 1882, C&GS sponsored the *USS Albatross,* built exclusively for fisheries and marine research. At Woods Hole, Massachusetts, in 1885 the Survey constructed the first marine fishery research laboratory. These government agencies brought focus to marine research.

In January 1902, industrialist Andrew Carnegie in the interest of science founded the Carnegie Institution of Washington. The endowment of $10 million dollars eclipsed the endowments at five Ivy League universities and was ten times greater than James Smithson's bequest to the United States ultimately leading to the Smithsonian Institute.[5] The Carnegie Institution authorized the construction of the wooden brigantine research ship *Carnegie* for making magnetic field measurements at sea. The vessel was commissioned in 1909 and widely used for research until 1929 when it was destroyed by fire. Throughout the 20th century and continuing into the new century, the Institution has steadily and broadly supported science research, including marine science.

Two small privately supported Marine Biological Laboratories were conducting marine research, one at Woods Hole, Massachusetts (1888) and one in La Jolla, California (1903). As late as the 1930s, " ... both were small, isolated institutions, each with staffs of about a dozen people, one ship, and limited research facilities."[6]

The California laboratory became part of the University of California in 1912 and the name was changed to Scripps Institution of Oceanography (SIO) in 1925 to reflect a broadened research focus. The Navy Hydrographic office supported research projects at SIO as early as 1920. In 1931, SIO had one main laboratory building, one small research vessel, a staff of twenty-six, and an unsteady annual budget of $75,000.

In 1930, the Woods Hole laboratory filed articles of incorporation for the Woods Hole Oceanographic Institution (WHOI). Half of the support for Scripps came from the University of California while the Rockefeller Foundation was the principal patron for WHOI. Both institutes needed multiple sources of support.

Willard Bascom, noted scientist and oceanographer, observed "Until World War II, American oceanography consisted mainly of a few marine biologists based at the Scripps Institution of Oceanography in La Jolla, California and the Woods Hole Oceanographic Institution in Massachusetts.[7]

Prior to substantial direct support for oceanography by the Navy during WWII, Hydrographer Admiral Walter R. Gherardi provided WHOI and SIO with seawater temperature, salinity, and dynamic-sounding data gathered by the Hydrographic Office crews. In the 1930s, SIO scientists conducted research on board Hydrographic vessels.[8]

WWII operational requirements for surface ships, submarines, and naval aircraft (weather needs) created extensive and time-urgent needs by the Navy for oceanographic assistance. This wartime oceanographic support by the marine scientists heavily contributed to naval victory during the four-year war.

By mid-century, both WHOI and SOI became significant laboratories and known nationally and internationally. Before 1930 the number of United States oceanographers was about six.[9] Prior to WWII, the Hydrographic Office was the primary government agency interacting with private marine research. The onset of the war marked the beginning of a substantial involvement with the Navy and the marine laboratories which continued for the remainder of the century.

Marvin Lasky, in a review of scientific effort for ASW, 1939-1945, points out "Prior to 1939 technical people in the field of underwater sound probably numbered fewer than 150; by 1945 more than 3,000 were involved."[10]

Peace in 1945 did not end the Navy's need for further information about the seas. Shortly after several years of an uneasy peace, international politics and technological innovations applicable to ships, submarines, aircraft, and weapons collectively brought additional high priority Navy requirements for knowledge about the sea. Answers were found in the expanding multidisciplinary field of oceanography. At this time, the number of people trained to be oceanographers was limited. Oceanography was growing and the Navy supported its development.

In the last half of the 20th Century, the Korean, Vietnam, and escalating Cold War deepened the important relationship between the Navy and the oceanographic community. During this time, oceanography grew in importance to the Navy. Last century project names such as

AMOS, CAESAR, CROSSROADS, HEARLD, LOFAR, JEZEBEL, SOFAR and SOSUS are some examples of Navy-Oceanographic joint efforts. In addition to in-house Navy laboratories, private oceanographic laboratories and university support, the role of industrial activities in the implementation of these projects was significant.

Oceanographic Needs

World War I (WWI) and the introduction of successful submarine operations especially by the German U-boats against navies and merchant shipping initiated a strong interest in the characteristics of the sea below in pursuit of sound detection as a potential weapon against the submarine. The surface ships pursuing the submarine and the submarine in search of targets needed the then-unknown characteristics of the seas and the paths of sound in the sea.

Mutual trust and understanding between the marine scientists and the Navy grew throughout the century but not rapidly. A time line of the relationship shows a gradual increase in joint efforts during the 1920s and 30s, a huge common effort during WWII with an adjustment period during the immediate postwar years. By mid-20th century, the body of knowledge about the ocean's characteristics was no longer fragmentary and a scientific discipline known as oceanography was developing. Then in 1954 the nuclear submarine, new high technology weapons, and international tensions, Cold War, and Vietnam War brought increased Navy need for oceanography.

World War I (1914-18)

The enormous success of the German U-boat throughout the war established the submarine as a successful weapon in several regards. The submarines were small in size and crew requirements and effective. In February 1917,

225

with 150 U-boats and unrestricted warfare, the Germans were sinking one of every four merchant ships leaving England. As the war ended, there was no assured countermeasure for submarines. In 1917, the depth charge, the convoy system, the mine and seamanship were the basis for antisubmarine warfare (ASW).[11]

In 1915, George Ellery Hale a member of the National Academy of Sciences (NAS), recognized the significant success of the German U-boats. To accelerate antisubmarine warfare effort in the United States, then a noncombatant, with President Wilson's approval, Hale set up a partnership between science and industry in the military that accelerated the antisubmarine warfare effort.

To facilitate this, NAS in June 1916 established the National Research Council (NRC). For the first time, the Council brought scientists and engineers from industry and academia to address a broad array of challenges related to upgrading military preparedness prior to and following the April 1917 entry of the United States in the war. On May 11, 1918, President Wilson signed an executive order providing for the Council's perpetuation in peacetime.[12]

The NRC from its inception continuously backed Navy underwater interests in a variety of ways. Through the years, this assistance came primarily in the form of a respected and listened-to scientific voice in the Washington arena where Congressional fiscal support for science-related work was frequently critical. During the mid-1920s, NRC's science support was helpful. The NRC organized according to fields of science, not around the administrative and scientific problems of government.[13] Navy oceanographic needs found positive support from the Council for the rest of the 20th century. The NRC has been referred to as the operating arm of the NAS.[14]

Wartime antisubmarine research and experience pointed to further investigation of underwater sound as a tool for detection of enemy submarines. The need for more accurate data about the sea was required.

Interwar Years

In the 1920s, government agency support for marine science usually had an applied practical aspect: safety at sea, making maps, and the needs of the fishing industry. Privately supported marine scientists' orientation was in basic research. Modest post- WWI interest stemmed in part from the successful U-boat performance mentioned above and the realization that detailed knowledge about the sea environment was lacking. Primary Navy interest was in underwater detection of enemy submarines. In addition to federal involvement, support for marine research came from business, private sources, and academic interest. The 1920s were also marked by a significant reduction in federal funding following the end of the war. Historically, it is almost a tradition to reduce military funding following the end of a war.

During the 1920s and 1930s, work related to the Navy's continuing interest in the underwater detection of enemy submarines was at the newly constructed (1923) Naval Research Laboratory (NRL) in Anacostia, Maryland and the Submarine Signal Company of Boston. The work started during WWI on radio signaling and submarine detection provided a basis for NRL's primary mission to perform applied research and support naval operations. The scientists and technicians who worked there were primarily civilians.[15]

Between the World Wars, three important nautical instruments were introduced. Each device provided new information about the seas. Sound detection and echo ranging equipment required extensive knowledge regarding the propagation of sound in the sea. The navy began cooperative work with oceanographic institutions.

Detection equipment performance gradually revealed the impact of the various properties of the sea, sea life and topography on system performance. For the Navy, particular oceanographic knowledge was a prerequisite for best operational use of the evolving equipment.

The U.S. Navy's WWII operational requirements around the world for surface ships, submarines, and naval aircraft (weather) created extensive and time critical need for expanded oceanographic assistance. This wartime oceanographic support provided by the scientists contributed significantly to naval victory during the four-year war.[16]

During WWII, system development and implementation were heavily influenced by important participation by physicists and oceanographic (marine science) personnel. Marine scientists participation included going to sea on Navy as well as laboratory ships in addition to laboratory effort. In the post-war era, both professions were heavily pursued and the number of universities offering marine science and related fields of study increased.

New Instrumentation

Successful U-boat operation during WWI against the merchant and naval shipping encouraged continued investigation of submarine detection using sound. Results of testing the newly developed equipment pointed towards oceanographic investigation to find answers to problems having to do with attenuation of sound in seawater and other related topics. The surface ships pursuing the enemy submarine and the submarine in search of targets required more information about the then-unknown characteristics of the seas and the paths of sound in the ocean.

Sonic Depth Finder (Fathometer)

The Fathometer and the Bathythermograph (BT) contributed to the collection of data about the sea. The efficiency of data collection and the amount of data collected was improved by orders of magnitude. Measuring the depth of the ocean was always demanding and labor intensive and the measurement of great depths not always feasible.

The 1920 device for depth measurement had its beginnings in a 1913 acoustic oscillator patent application by Reginald A. Fessenden.

In 1914, Fessenden installed his oscillator on the United States Revenue cutter *Miami* while on the first International Iceberg Patrol operating on the Grand Banks off Newfoundland, Canada. The oscillator was suspended underwater from the side of the *Miami* and for three hours successfully received underwater echoes from an iceberg 430 feet long and 130 feet high.

Harvey C. Hayes

Hayes, a physics professor from Swarthmore College, developed underwater submarine detection equipment during WWI at the NRC's Fort Trumbull laboratory at New London, Connecticut (1917-18). When the WWI ended he continued his investigations, initially at the Annapolis, Maryland Naval Engineering Experiment Station and then in 1923 at the new Navy Research Laboratory (NRL) in Anacostia, Maryland.

In 1922 at Annapolis, Hayes developed a sonic depth finder (SDF) based on his work in 1918 at New London, The sound source for the echo ranging was a Fessenden 540 Hz oscillator developed and demonstrated earlier in 1914. An MV hydrophone, invented by Max Mason at New London during WWI, was used for reception. The MV is a non-electric binaural listening system. The Hayes depth finder also included a timing device to determine the time interval; from that the distance from the source to the target could be determined.[17]

Depth finder performance was further enhanced by the tables Hayes developed to assist the depth finder operator to quickly determine the depth from the observed data. "A single deep-ocean sounding with line and sinker had taken a better part of a day: with the Hayes Sonic Depth Finder sounding could be executed in a minute."[18] The finder evolved into the Fathometer patented and manufactured by the Submarine Signal Company of Boston. Within a few years, Fathometers were widely used by merchant shipping and navies. By 1929, the U.S. Hydrographic Office received daily reports of deep-sea soundings.

During the period June 22-29, 1922, Hayes on board the destroyer *U.S.S. Stewart* (DD224) equipped with a Navy SDF made the first continuous profile of 900 deep-sea soundings to depths greater than 3000 feet[19] across the entire ocean basin from Newport, Rhode Island, to the Azores, and then to Gibraltar. Hayes left the destroyer at Gibraltar. Next the destroyer, without interfering with the destroyer's routine, continued on to China Station, and taking a total of 6500 nautical miles of continuous soundings.[20]

The ease of the sonic soundings by the *Stewart*, contrasting with an earlier effort by the *HMS Challenger* using line and sinker demonstrates the huge advantage of the Hayes equipment. The marine exploration vessel *HMS Challenger* in a cruise of about four years (1872-76) made 300 soundings every 100 miles using line and sinker. The *Stewart's* rapid profiling introduced a new dimension in gathering data about the ocean depths. At the 1904 VIII International Geophysical Congress in Washington, DC a sound chart plotted 18,400 points; by 1932 the number was 370,000.[21]

The Fathometer, in addition to much improved efficiency in measuring depth, provided a way to reveal the undersea contours and greatly helped the underwater cable laying industry, reducing cable slack required by half. Before WWII, private marine scientists using fathometers to investigate submarine topography and marine geological processes found financial support from petroleum companies.[22]

Hayes Memorandum

Hayes, aware of the decreased fiscal support for the Navy following the end of WWI, felt strongly that congressional support for NRL was critical for continuing his wartime research in the use of underwater sound to detect enemy submarines. He addressed these issues in a February 19, 1923 memorandum citing the value of oceanographic research to advance maritime safety and naval operations. He cited the political, economic and scientific value of oceanography.[23] Along with scientists from other government agencies Hayes made an effort to establish an oceanographic office within the Navy but failed for lack of financial support.[24]

With his status as a scientist, his recent development of the SDF followed by his at-sea depth measurements made his memorandum credible. Hayes clearly pointed out the value to the Navy of more science orientation and a convivial approach to the marine science community members to work towards common goals jointly. While the memorandum did not result in the creation of an oceanographic office, it did have beneficial effects.

Congressional and public awareness to the Navy and marine science was raised. In August 1923, U.S. Navy participation in a Pan-Pacific Science Congress in Australia included sending the new light cruiser *Milwaukee* (CL5) using the SDF en route to make a series of ocean bottom profiles and to present the findings at the Congress.[25]

The following year, under the aegis of the NRC and others, a federal Interagency Conference on Oceanography was held to determine the nature of naval commitment to oceanographic research for the next two decades. The planning included a positive attitude toward cooperative oceanographic work with the Navy by the private oceanographic sector.

An increase in joint civilian and Navy oceanic research followed this heightened awareness about marine science, but it did not grow rapidly until WWII and beyond. Basic sea research with modest fiscal support during the interwar years provided useful information about the performance of underwater detection equipment. In some of the areas researched, including salinity, hydrostatic pressure, turbulence, air bubbles, and temperature gradients, knowledge grew.[26] The global scale of the coming war quickly indicated the importance of oceanography and the operational needs of the military that included more than the underwater detection requirements.

Navy-Princeton Gravity Expedition 1932

At that time, there was interest in making gravity measurements at sea to increase knowledge about the earth's underlying structure. A submarine was suitable for the instrumentation available to make measurements. Measurements from surface craft were hampered by surface wave action. The Navy provided the submarine S48 for six weeks of measurements from February 7 to March 17, 1932.

With civilian scientists aboard, gravity measurements were made in the region of the West Indies. Submarine gravity measurements at depths in excess of 100 feet used a gimbaled multiple pendulum device gravimeter. Submarine gravimeters were in use from 1923-1950. Hyman Rickover on a three-year tour was the executive officer and navigator.[27] By mid century, surface ship equipment for gravity subsurface measurements was available.

Later in the century with underwater missile launches aimed at targets thousands of miles away, gravity variations assumed significant importance. "Knowing gravity variations helps a submarine stay on course when it is underwater and sailing blind, and when the time comes to launch a missile…that knowledge is essential."[28]

1936-37 Crucial Oceanographic Events

Bathythermograph

Understanding how the ocean moves and mixes heat requires accurate and continuous measurements of temperature as it changes with depth. With this in mind, in the summer of 1934, Carl Rosby a summer resident of Woods Hole and Massachusetts Institute of Technology (MIT) meteorologist, constructed and took to sea aboard the *Atlantis* (the Woods Hole oceanographic research vessel) a boxlike structure, an oceanograph, designed to record continuous tracings of temperature versus depth in the surface layers of the ocean. The objective was to be an improvement over the current methods for measurement.[29]

The device consisted of a compressible bellows with a pen arm and a stylus at one end. The stylus moved horizontally to temperature changes and rested on a smoked–glass slide recording the changes. Vertical stylus movement recorded depth.[30] Rosby gave the device to Athelstan Spilhaus at MIT to redesign. By 1937, a Spilhaus-patented prototype called a bathythermograph (BT) was available to go aboard the *Atlantis*.

The BT soon evolved into an important device for surface ships seeking enemy submarines and equally desirable for submarines in avoiding detection. Thousands were manufactured during WWII. They were classified secret for some period after the end of the war.

USS Semmes (AG 24)

In late 1936, the *Semmes* (a 1919 destroyer) was converted to a research and experimental sound vessel attached to the Navy Research Laboratory. It was equipped with highly classified underwater sound echo-ranging gear (sonar) and working with a submarine out of Guantanamo Bay Naval Base in Cuba. An abnormal operating condition with the equipment was encountered. The equipment worked well every morning. Later in the day, with the *Semmes* steaming right over the target submarine no detection was made. When the Semmes returned to New London, Connecticut (the ship's homeport), Lieutenant William Pryor of the *Semmes* took the problem to the director of WHOI. The Institute was interested and arranged to conduct almost two weeks of joint testing with the *Semmes*, the *Atlantis*, and a submarine early in 1937 near Guantanamo, Cuba. Additional tests were made following August off Long Island. Institute underwater sound and submarine detection experiments continued into 1940.

Columbus Iselin, the assistant director at WHOI, participated in the test and his conclusions were seminal. He put forward that the sonar problem stemmed from the way sound traveled through water and the layers of cooler and warmer water near the surface caused bending and distortion of the sound beam. The phenomenon was called "afternoon effect." The about-to-be patented and improving BT with the capability to provide a record of the depth and temperature certainly loomed on the horizon as an important tool to assist the submarine hunter (the surface ship) and the target submarine to successfully hide from the searching hunter. Research pointed to temperature and pressure as two main variables influencing underwater sound transmission.[31]

A noteworthy aspect of this 1937 successful cooperative venture by the Navy and Woods Hole laboratory was that it marked the beginning of a continuing relationship between the Navy and the marine science community as it grew in the years leading up to WWII. The Navy considered water temperature of the upper layers critical information. By 1940, expedited and expanded effort vastly improved the

BT for use from moving surface ships and later for use on submarines.[32]

Maurice Ewing

On October 17, 1937, geophysics professor Ewing from Lehigh University joined Columbus Iselin aboard the *Atlantis* for a test cruise. His interest was to conduct seismic refraction experiments to determine the thickness and makeup of sediments at the ocean bottom at depths of three miles in the North Atlantic. He used underwater explosives (10 pound TNT blocks) as sound sources and noted that a chain of echoes was generated by repeated reflections between the ocean bottom and the sea surface especially at the lower frequencies and traveled long distance underwater with limited loss. Further, if hydrophones were carefully located in this <u>deep sound channel</u> the signals could be detected. Important implementation of this channel identification followed but not immediately.

Endnotes

[1] Brenda Horsfield, Peter Bennet Stone, *The Great Ocean Business*, Houder & Stoughton, Toronto, Ontario, 1972, p. 11.

[2] Vicky Cullen, *Down to the Sea for Science*, Woods Hole Oceanographic Institution, Woods Hole, MA, 2005, p. 14.

[3] Susan Schlee, *The Edge of an Unfamiliar World*, Dutton, NY, 1973, p. 79

[4] George A. W. Boehm, The Explorer of "Inner Space," Fortune, November 1980, p. 163.

[5] Susan Schlee, *op. cit.*, p266.

[6] Ronald Rainger, "Science at the Crossroads: The Navy, Bikini Atoll, and American Oceanography in the 1940s," http://repositories.edlib.org/cgi/viewcontent.cgi?article=1004&context=sio/arch p. 2 (Also see: Historical Studies in the Physical and Biological Sciences 30(2); p. 349-371.)

[7] Willard Bascom, *The Crest of the Wave: Adventures in Oceanography*, Harper & Row, NY, 1988, p. xiii.

[8] Ronald Rainger, *op. cit.*, p. 2.

[9] Rexmond C. Cochrane, *The National Academy of Sciences: The First Hundred Years 1863-1963*, National Academy of Sciences, D.C., 1978, p. 502.

[10] Marvin Lasky, "A Review of Scientific Effort for Undersea Warfare: 1939-1945," U.S. Navy Journal of Underwater Acoustics, Vol. 25, No. 3, July 1975, p. 567.

[11] A. Hunter Dupree, *Science in the Federal Government: A History of Policies and activities to 1940*, Belknap Press of Harvard University Press, Cambridge, Massachusetts, 1957, p. 319.

[12] John Merrill, "From the Heavens to the Depths," Naval History, Vol. 14, No. 3, June 2000, p. 58,59.

[13] Gary Weir, *op. cit.*, p. 352.

[14] Willard Bascom, *op. cit.*, p. 171.

[15] Susan Schlee, *op. cit.*, p. 250.

[16] ibid, p. 281.

[17] ibid, p. 250.

[18] Robert Kunzig, *The Restless Sea: Exploring the World Beneath the Waves*, W.W. Norton & Company, NY, 1999, p. 18.

[19] Gary E. Weir, "Surviving the Peace: The Advent of American Naval Oceanography," http://www.nwc.navy.mil/press/Review/1997/autumn/art6-a97.htm, p. 5.

[20] Thomas H. Whitcroft, "Sonic Sounding: As Developed by the U.S. Navy," Naval Institute Proceedings, February 1943, p. 220.

[21] Brenda Horsfield, Peter Bennet Stone, *op. cit.*, p. 51.

[22] Ronald Rainger, *op. cit.*, p. 7.

[23] Gary Weir, *An Ocean in Common: American Naval Officers, Scientists, and the Ocean Environment*, Texas A&M University Press, College Station, TX, 2001, p. 28.

[24] Ronald Rainger, *op. cit.*, p. 24.

[25] Gary Weir, *op. cit.*, p. 18.

[26] Willem Hackmann, *Seek and Strike: Sonar, anti-submarine warfare and the Royal navy 1914-54*, London: Her Majesty's Stationery Office, 1984, p. 152.

[27] "A Seagoing Sailor at Last,"http://ttbrown.com/defying_gravity/26_asailoratlast.html

[28] Robert Kunzig, *op. cit.*, p. 67.

[29] Vicki Cullen, *op. cit.*, p. 56.

[30] Susan Schlee, *The Edge of an Unfamiliar World*, Dutton, NY, 1973, p. 290.

[31] Ronald Rainger, *op. cit.*, p. 3.

[32] Susan Schlee, On Almost any Wind: the Saga of the Oceanographic Research Vessel "Atlantis", Cornell University Press, Ithaca, NY, 197

U.S. Navy and 20th Century Oceanography:

Summary 1900-1960Part II

World War II

17 Months before Pearl Harbor

In May 1940, Vannevar Bush, former dean of the MIT School of Engineering and currently president of the Carnegie Institution of Washington, proposed to President Franklin D. Roosevelt the concept of a National Defense Research Committee (NDRC) to coordinate, supervise, and conduct scientific research for war purposes except for flight. On June 15, 1940, the day after the fall of France, President Roosevelt signed the letter of appointment of the twelve members of the Committee and selected Bush as chairman. The NDRC was established June 27, 1940 under the National Defense Act of 1916. This was seventeen months before Pearl Harbor.

During the summer of 1940, director of WHOI, Columbus Iselin and president of Bell Laboratories. F. B. Jewett, a member of NAS, and a director of the newly formed NDRC, concluded that a way of predicting the performance of echo sounders (sonar) was essential and that oceanographers were best suited to work on the problem. NDRC initiated contracts with Woods Hole. Within a year the staff grew from 60 to about 300 with the budget increasing from $135,000 to almost $1,000,000.[33] Iselin's pre-war initiatives included collaborative efforts with U. S. Coast Guard oceanographers.

NDRC awarded one of its first contracts to WHOI to investigate transmission of sound in the sea. By October the Institute's first year-round staff was brought together to work on that project and others. In February 1941, Iselin and Ewing completed the study and report, "Sound Transmission in Sea Water."

It was "a treatise on a new and unexplored subject-submarine acoustics. Not only did it set down what was then known about the transmission of sound underwater (and this was later incorporated into manuals for sonar operators), it also pointed out what remained to be learned."[34] At this time San Diego destroyer personnel were questioning the interpretation of how oceanographic conditions affected sonar performance.[35] In addition to the sound transmission study, in September the Navy sponsored a two-year program at WHOI to broadly investigate underwater sound and its propagation over a wide band of detection frequencies.

A second NDRC contract with Woods Hole in 1940 involved the development of undersea instrumentation. Maurice Ewing, at Woods Hole from 1940-44, with others took over BT development and made it an improved and more efficient instrument.

Columbia, Harvard and California University Underwater Sound Laboratories

On June 27, 1940, the day the NDRC was established, Secretary of the Navy Frank Knox asked the NAS to appoint a committee to advise him on the scientific aspects of defense against submarines and the adequacy of the Navy's preparations. In late March 1941, the advice of the NAS committee's findings, Colpitts Report, was brought to the General Board of the Navy. The findings quickly established the urgent need for broad scientific and engineering investigations to develop equipment and methods essential in submarine and subsurface warfare. An April 10, 1941 letter to Vannevar Bush asked the NDRC to undertake an investigation of submarine detection.

> **Woods Hole Institute of Oceanography WWII***
> Bathythermograph development for use aboard submarines
> Investigation and development of Ewing's "Sound Channel"
> Studies to predict sea and surf conditions for amphibious operations
> Studies of low level meteorological phenomena related to aircraft
> carrier operations and laying smoke screens
> Study of antifouling paints and fouling organisms for the Bureau of ships
>
> *Office of Scientific Research & Development 5 contracts $2,110,000[36]

By July 1941, Columbia, California, and Harvard universities were under NDRC contract to immediately establish civilian laboratories "to function as centers for research on **underwater acoustics** and the design and construction of underwater sound equipment. The Navy had responsibility for all testing and development of such equipments and weapons."[37] The initial NDRC contracts and the follow-on negotiations covered the following four years of war.

At the end of WWII, in addition to the wartime technical contributions of the three university laboratories to ASW, some of the laboratory personnel became a core group of scientists and engineers that addressed the submarine problem (pro and anti) viewpoint at government, academic, and industrial activities. Pennsylvania, Washington, and Texas State Universities were some of the locations that continued pursuing the submarine problem. The New London and San Diego laboratory facilities provided the starting point for continuing civilian-led Navy R&D.

The Columbia University Division of War Research (CUDWR) primary site was a laboratory in proximity to the Navy Submarine Base on U. S. Coast Guard property at Fort Trumbull in New London, Connecticut. By 1944, the civilian scientific and non-scientific staff peaked at 330. In addition, 36 officers and 295 enlisted personnel were assigned to the laboratory primarily to man the assigned Navy test vessels. All the university laboratories had ships available to conduct sea tests.

Columbia University's civilian scientific staff at Fort Trumbull grew to130 by 1944. Engineers were predominant with physicists comprising about ten percent. About one-third came from colleges and universities and represented 25 states

University of California's (UCDWR) contract eventually brought a staff of about 550 to the Navy installation at Point Loma in San Diego, California to pursue antisubmarine research and development including projects on cavitation, attenuation, and underwater noise. Scripps Oceanographic Institute located fifteen miles north of Point Loma provided several oceanographers to the new laboratory and the proximity allowed further cooperative efforts with UCDWR.[38]

NDRC contracted with Harvard on June 5, 1942 and the Harvard Underwater Sound Laboratory (HUSL) began with the primary activity in Cambridge, Massachusetts. The staff peaked in August 1944 with a total of 462 and additional facilities including a field-testing station in Fort Lauderdale, Florida. F. V. Hunt director of the Harvard Underwater Sound Laboratory 1941-46 originated the word "sonar" in 1942.

WWII Oceanographic Interests

Prewar oceanography encouraged work in all fields. WWII, with emphasis on subsurface and amphibious warfare emphasized physical, chemical and geological oceanography. Defensive and offensive warfare looked to oceanography for answers and direction. Navy support for WHOI and SOI escalated to resolve significant oceanographic problems. The normal summertime staff at WHOI at 60 increased to a year-round staff of 335; at Scripps and UCDWR the number increased by several hundred.[39]

Sea Mines

Navies of the world were alerted to the value of sea mines beginning in 1904 with Japan's successful use of fields of mines during the short Russo-Japanese War. In the much longer WWI, mines were broadly used in incredibly large numbers and in different ways. Germany successfully mined and blocked the Bosporus during the Gallipoli campaign. WWI demonstrated mine ASW capability. During WWII, the mine was again an essential weapon.

Mines are a dual challenge. Planting them as a defensive measure and detecting and destroying mines as a protective one brings about a need for answers to oceanographic questions. Ocean bottom sediment knowledge is addressed when planting mines or when detecting or destroying mines. In the case of harbor protection, detecting their presence is the challenge. Information was needed to understand the bottom penetration of mines dropped by planes and surface ships. Further, what would be the impact of underwater currents and surface wave action on the movement of the mine? Could sediment coloration camouflage enhance mine performance? Oceanographers addressed and answered these questions along with others.

Harbor protection focused on passive detection of ships, submarines and weapons including mines. Detecting mines in shallow water required bottom sedimentary information. In support of Pacific operations in late 1943, Hydrographic Office vessels *U.S.S. Bowditch* and the *U.S.S. Cape Johnson* carried out dredging, soundings and BT profiles at all islands and atolls.[40]

Antifouling Project

Improved marine paint from the antifouling paint research sponsored by the Bureau of Ships at WHOI cited above provided a great number of benefits during the war years. Fouled paint slows ships and increases fuel consumption. Fouling reduction reduces shipyard time. In addition to ship's hulls, buoys, anchors, chains, amphibious aircraft, and ships saltwater piping systems also benefit. Later in reporting on the antifouling investigation the Navy noted "...project increased the overall efficiency of their ships 10% during the war years."[41]

Sonar Charts

At the beginning of the war, BTs were not available in great numbers and needed improvements, including a submarine version. To counter this shortage, WHOI and SOI created charts to aid ship's officers and sonar operators in strategically locations. At SOI, extensive existing Japanese data regarding temperature and salinity of the near islands of Japan were used. At SIO and CUDWR sediment charts of eastern and SE continental shelves of Asia were created from 400,000 bottom notations based on Japanese lead line and bottom sampling data. At WHOI, around 60,000 bathythermograph records of shallow water profiles obtained in the North Atlantic were reduced to monthly charts of temperature to a depth of 200 meters.[42]

Bathythermograph Development

During the war, the BT became standard equipment on all U.S. Navy submarines and vessels involved in ASW. Improvements made the BT capable of being deployed and retrieved from a surface ship moving at fifteen to twenty knots. Independently, Ewing at WHOI and Revelle at CUDWR at Point Loma developed slide rules to speed computing echo ranges and making echo range predictions from BT data.

The BT for use on a submarine provided sound transmission and ballasting data. Initial production of BTs, BT winches and SBTs (submarine BT) took place at WHOI along with BT training for USN ensigns.[43] Submarine Signal Company of Boston became involved in the production of the BT needed on destroyers, destroyer escorts, and some navy transports in addition to submarines. Oceanographers and physicists worked aboard ships and submarines in the training of Navy operators on BTs, sonar and other new systems and instruments.

Wave Prediction

U.S. military planning amphibious attacks required oceanographic information on wave and surf forecasting, beaches, shorelines and coasts. In 1942, SIO was asked to study the problem of predicting surf conditions. The work supported Operation Torch, the trans-Atlantic invasion of Vichy French North Africa planned for October of that year.

At Scripps the useful concept of significant wave height and periods evolved. Oceanographers started by creating wind maps and observing the connection between wind patterns and swell size. By 1945, oceanographic and geophysics personnel had been consulted regarding the kind of landing craft and surf conditions best for making landings and securing beachheads.[44] "If during the war, the greatest number of oceanographers worked to solve problems related to submarine warfare, then certainly the next greatest number were concerned with amphibious warfare."[45]

The Navy's Hydrographic Office in 1943 was tasked to furnish relevant oceanographic information to military services in all part of the world. In preparation for the 1944 invasion of Normandy, a network of 51 wave-reporting stations was established along the south and southeast coast of England. Similar steps were taken for the invasions of Burma and Indonesia.

A Sound Pipeline

At WHOI in 1942, Maurice Ewing with J. L. Worzel resumed work on "deep sound channel" signal propagation proposed by Ewing in1937. Ewing theorized that low-frequency waves, which are less vulnerable than higher frequencies to scattering and absorption, should be able to travel great distances if the sound source is placed correctly. Ewing theorized that low-frequency waves, which are less vulnerable than higher frequencies to scattering and absorption, should be able to travel great distances, if the sound source is placed correctly. In analyzing the results of this test, they discovered a kind of sound pipeline, which they called Sound Fixing and Ranging (SOFAR), channel, also known as the "deep sound channel."[46]

An additional test was conducted in the spring of 1944 aboard the research vessel *R/V Saluda* operating in the vicinity of Eleuthera in the Bahamas. A deep receiving hydrophone was hung from *R/V Saluda*. A Navy ship dropped 4-pound explosive charges set to explode at 4000 feet in the ocean at distances up to 900 miles from the *R/V Saluda's* hydrophone. The Navy ship's operations were limited to this distance. Receivers located in Dakar on the west coast of Africa easily detected the underwater explosions at a range of the order of 3,200 km (2000 miles). Ewing and Worzel heard, for the first time, the characteristic sound of a SOFAR transmission, consisting of a series of pulses building up to its climax.[47]

During the war, an application of Ewing's deep sound channel involved setting up coastal hydrophones to listen for the sound bursts from small explosives set off by pilots downed at sea to provide bearings for their location and retrieval. It was not until 1947 that permanent listing stations were ready for use.[48] Ewing's deep-water channel discovery provided a basis for the mid-century Sound Surveillance System (SOSUS) widely used during the Cold War.

Navigation System

A NOAA summary of the electronics (1923-1945) asserts: "Perhaps the most important innovation to come out of the war, however, was the evolution of electronic navigation systems as an outgrowth of radar development. These navigation systems were used for precision aerial bombing navigation, but by the end of the war, both the British and U. S. Coast and Geodetic Survey were using them to conduct hydrographic surveys."[49] It should be noted that the Loran radio navigation system developed at MIT during the war has also been cited as providing a significant navigational tool for the oceanographic community.

The oceanographic work at Woods Hole, the University of California Laboratory at Point Loma, Scripps at La Jolla, and Columbia University at New London, Connecticut heavily contributed directly to naval warfare and also advanced the basic understanding of the ocean environment. In addition, the participation of colleges, universities and industry should not be overlooked.

AFTER WWII

Peace in 1945 did not end the Navy's requirements for further information about the seas. Shortly after several years of an uneasy peace, international politics and technological innovations applicable to ships, submarines, aircraft, and weapons collectively brought additional high priority Navy oceanographic needs. Encouragement to continue advancing ASW tactics and systems was stimulated when the details of German submarine developments near the end of the war were recognized. Increased underwater submarine speed and the schnorkel provided new challenges with oceanographic implications. Interest in submarine operating depths of 1000 feet became a consideration.

The arrival of the nuclear submarine in 1954 followed by the Polaris submarines brought additional oceanographic questions to be addressed such as the global topography of the ocean's bottoms, seamounts, maps of the sea floor, earth's magnetic field, gravity, and bottom contours. By 1980, the Navy was spending most of $20 million on oceanography, an extremely expensive science as noted in <u>Fortune</u> of November 1980. The nuclear submarine's operating depths and long underwater capability and a potential enemy with a long coastline on the Arctic Ocean made under-ice operations a reality with major oceanographic significance and additional oceanographic needs.

Research Support

With the end of the war, many marine scientists returned to prewar status at universities and private industry. Private science and government science boundaries reappeared. Fiscal support for oceanography or related research government support was encouraged at oceanographic institutions. At this time, NRC, the active arm of the NAS, perceived a need to encourage continuation of wartime anti and pro submarine research by establishing a Committee on Undersea Warfare.

In the evolution of the place and direction of United States science research in post WWII, respected and successful wartime head of the NDRC and Office of Research and Development Vannevar Bush, strongly advocated, "Civilian scientists should work in parallel with the military, but not within the Services."[50] Washington took note of his discussions and writings. The two new government agencies discussed below in some ways reflect Bush's views in their organization and goals.

The new Office of Naval Research (ONR) established in August 1946 and the National Science Foundation (NSF) created in 1950 by an Act of Congress provided a national environment for the support of science in the United States. In 1949 prior to the advent of NSF, ONR was the principal supporter of fundamental research by U.S. scientists. This was in addition to its military research employing 1000 scientists at three naval laboratories.[51] The successes of federally-sponsored oceanographic research and U.S. leadership that followed was due in part to government-university-industry relationships engendered by ONR and NSF. By 1969, federal interest and substantial support brought new oceanographic vessels, new laboratories, and universities and colleges having courses in oceanography.

Office of Naval Research (ONR)

Initially ONR broadly supported science. NSF's creation in 1950 with extensive funds to support a variety of scientific endeavors caused ONR to focus more heavily on supporting oceanographic research. Three of the country's leading oceanographic institutions (WHOI, SIO and Columbia University's Lamont-Doherty Geological Observatory, founded in 1956) depended heavily on ONR support. ONR turned out to be an exemplary military patron of marine science research.

ONR addressed fundamental problems, basic and applied, particularly in physical oceanography and geochemistry. Support by ONR included academic research ships and development of new tools and instruments. Between 1946 and 1965, the Navy provided 80 to 90 percent of the funding for American research in oceanography. The breadth of ONR's contractors' autonomy is seen in an ONR 1959 contract with SIO that promised, "to permit investigation of all phases of oceanography."

National Science Foundation (NSF)

Looking to the future, success in WWII from wartime scientific research indicated that continuing support for scientific research was essential to national defense and welfare. With the National Science Foundation Act of 1950, Congress established the Foundation as the role of advisor to the government to promote the advancement of science in all its branches regardless of its applications. It is the only federal agency whose mandate includes science and engineering research and education at all levels and across all fields. NSF organization was modeled after the successful ONR.

NSF has direct access to Congress for funds. The researching organizations contracting with NSF meet the criterion of not being subject to control or direction from any operating organizations whose responsibilities are not exclusively those of research.[52]

The NSF assumed major federal responsibility for developing academic and institutional capability in ocean science research in the sixties. Ocean science programs were established at John Hopkins University, Texas A. & M., Oregon State, University of Miami, Rhode Island, and others. In the 1970s, the Navy in-house program had no fewer than 34 ships in its ocean science program with 18 academic and private institutions engaged in Navy-sponsored work.[53]

Sputnik October 4, 1957

This success of Soviet technology's Sputnik marked the starting point of a technology race for space with overtones for oceanography in the United States. NSF'S budget growing slowly from its establishment in 1950 doubled two years after Sputnik. Two significant documents appeared during the two years post Sputnik: the Navy's oceanographic needs and goals were made known in Ten Years in Oceanography and the National Academy of Sciences Committee on Oceanography landmark report Oceanography1960-1970. The NAS document assented to basic research, applied research and surveys. "The key to the growth of oceanography in the United States lies in basic research—research that is done for its own sake without the thought of practical application…"[54] Oceanography would be supported in the years ahead.

Submarines and Gravity

With ONR's support between 1947-55, scientists participated in conducting regional gravity surveys aboard Navy submarines in a variety of ocean locations. Columbia University's Lamont Laboratory personnel rode more than twenty boats over the nine-year period on two dozen separate gravity cruises. Submarines involved included *Dog* (SS-

401), *Bergall* (SS-320). *Archerfish* (SS-311), *Balao* ((SS-285), *Conger* (SS-477), *Corsair* (SS-435, *Diablo* (S-479) and *Toro* (S-422).[55]

A 1960 quote from director Maurice Ewing of the Lamont Laboratory ties the need for the gravity surveys to the newly-operational Navy submarine fired nuclear missile Regulus, "...These data are necessary for the precise direction of guided missiles."[56] Between the years 1952 and 1958 Regulus moved from experimental status to a fully operational weapon system. Regulus was installed on five missile submarines and eleven guidance submarines. During the Cold War years, the Regulus equipped submarines made more than 40 strategic deterrent patrols. With the advent of Fleet Ballistic Missile submarines in the 1960s, the Regulus submarines stopped operations 14 July 1964.

In 1995, the Navy declassified data concerning the earth's gravity that had been held secret. The Navy launched Geosat in 1985, on a near-polar orbit at 500 miles, to survey the altitude of the sea surface all over the world. This data provides information relative to sonar shadows and more importantly identifies gravity variations information essential to the submarine's staying on course while underwater and sailing blind. Most significantly, gravity information assists in setting an underwater-fired missile on the correct path to its target.[57]

Summary

The first half the 20th century gradually brought the Navy from a modest interest in marine science to a role in the last half as the primary supporter of oceanography in its broadest sense. The Navy's surface and subsurface constituencies required oceanographic support to be successful operationally.

The U-boat's success in WWI and WWII and its cours de guerre strategy contributed to the need for knowledge of the sea, the environment of submarines. WWII operations on all the oceans evoked attention to a variety of challenges in addition to those of special interest to submarines.

The 20th century with its overabundance of maritime wars and technology explosions that never ceased brought attention, focus, and fiscal support to marine science. Oceanography brought together two somewhat disparate professional groups, naval officers and marine scientists. Navy interest was invariably practical and looked for answers to ship operation questions. Marine scientists aimed at a careful search for new scientific knowledge about the sea. Common understanding had to be found. Navy officers whose career paths included strong oceanographic interests aided the search.

Endnotes

[33] ibid, p. 120..

[34] Susan Schlee, *The Edge of an Unfamiliar World*, Dutton, NY, 1973, p. 290, 292.

[35] Ronald Rainger, <u>Patronage and Science: Roger Revelle, the Navy, and Oceanography at the Scripps</u> Institution. Department of History, Texas Tech University, Lubbock, TX, 2000, p. 6; Weir *op. cit.*, p. 112.

[36] James Phinney Baxter, *Scientists Against Time*, MIT Press, Cambridge, MA, 1968, p. 256.

[37] Ronald Rainger, "Science at the Crossroads: "The Navy, Bikini Atoll, and American Oceanography in the 1940s," <u>http://repositories.edlib.org/cgi/viewcontent.cgi?article=1004&context=sio/arch</u> p. 5.

[38] Ronald Rainger, Patronage and Science: Roger Revelle, the Navy, and Oceanography at the Scripps Institution. Department of History, Texas Tech University, Lubbock, TX, 2000, p. 6, 10.

[39] Susan Schlee, *op. cit.,* p. 282.

[40] Ronald Rainger, "Science at the Crossroads: The Navy, Bikini Atoll, and American Oceanography in the 1940s," <u>http://repositories.edlib.org/cgi/viewcontent.cgi?article=1004&context=sio/arch</u> p. 7,8.

[41] Vicky Cullen, *op. cit.*, p. 62.

[42] National Academies Press, "Biographical Memoirs," National Academy of Sciences, Vol. 64, 1994, p. 174.

[43] Vicky Cullen, *op. cit.*, p. 57, 58.

[44] Ronald Rainger, *op. cit.,* p. 10.

[45] Susan Schlee, *op. cit.*, p. 304.

[46] National Academy of Sciences, "Beyond Discovery: Sounding out the Ocean's Secrets." p. 7; http://www.beyonddiscovery.org/content/view.article.asp?a=219

[47] "Science of Sound in the Sea," http://www.dosits.org/science/sndmoves/4a.htm

[48] Susan Schlee, *op. cit.,* p. 292.

[49] "Age of Electronics (1923-1945)." History of NOAA Ocean Exploration, http://www.oceanexplorer.noaa.gov/history/electronic/electronic.html

[50] Willem Hackmann, *op. cit.*, p. 256

[51] Scientific American, February 1949, p. 11.

[52] Rexmond C. Cochrane, *op. cit.*, p. 434.

[53] Brenda Horsfield, *op. cit.*, 180,181.

[54] Edward Wenk, *Politics of the Ocean*, Washington University Press, Seattle, WA, 1972, p. 43, 44.

[55] Gary Weir, *op. cit.*, p. 257.

[56] Gary Weir, *op. cit.*, p. 257.

[57] Robert Kunzig, *op. cit.*, 6

Remembering:

The Sound Surveillance System (SOSUS)*

Part I

*An aim of this paper is to bring some of the history of SOSUS that has been covered by various naval historians and others to an additional audience.

Introduction

SOSUS, initially an experimental and growing concept to provide long-range detection capability using the underwater propagation of low-frequency sound began, in 1950. SOSUS the classified name was established in 1952. The system became an exemplary Cold War tool. SOSUS arrays, along with nuclear submarines optimized for ASW and long-range maritime patrol craft, became the dominant tools in the U.S. Navy ASW posture in the mid and late 1950s.[1] It was strategic early warning.

Because SOSUS monitoring stations were fixed and shore-based, they were resistant to destruction, foul weather, and ambient self-generated noise. A SOSUS station consists of hydrophones mounted on the floor of the ocean and connected by cable to processing equipment ashore. The unprocessed data including ocean sounds and those of submarines are sent to processing centers for determination of whether they are a positive submarine contact. Appropriate action is then taken. Building and operating the early facilities, eventually almost on a global scale, with 1950 technology provided a significant challenge.

The system was still growing and improving during the late 1970s. After 41 years of service, in 1991 the system mission was declassified. The international setting for these SOSUS years included the Korean War, Cuban Missile crisis, Vietnam War, and the ever-present Cold War, SOSUS was developed, implemented, and operated under conditions of utmost secrecy. During its operation, there was continual and increasing pressure from a determined, highly competitive, and on occasion effective Cold War enemy. Furthermore, the ultimate global reach and scale of the system required unceasing effort to accommodate the shifting international scene. Complex challenges were omnipresent. System performance was improved with better technology.

The system's objective is to identify the general area where a submarine might be operating, filter out most man-made sounds and identify the acoustical wave from the submarine's engines and propellers. With this data, the bearing, depth, and distance to the source of the sound may be determined and identification of the source is possible. In addition to monitoring ocean noise, ships, submarines, noise from planes flying over the ocean and falling rain were identified. An oceanographer's comment about SOSUS in 1996 is appropriate, "It's unique. It's the only way to keep track of what goes on in the ocean."[2]

It is interesting to note that the oceanographic research and observations made in 1937 by Maurice Ewing in conducting seismic studies at the Woods Hole Oceanographic Institute (WHOI) provided the basis for the initial SOSUS installation in 1952. SOSUS technology consisted of hydrophones on long underwater cables laid along the shore leading to the continental shelf.

Considering advances in Antisubmarine Warfare (ASW), a 1980 remark is apt "…in both the Atlantic and the Pacific, SOSUS is capable of fixing the position on an enemy submarine within a radius of 50 nautical miles or less."[3] A later comment, 1986, made by an Massachusetts Institute of Technology assessment of a SOSUS satellite-linked capability "…at its best it can pinpoint the location of older (and therefore noisier) Soviet subs to within ten miles of their actual position from a distance of ten thousand miles, and that a twenty-five mile fix from "several thousand miles: is feasible in most cases."[4]

Examining the SOSUS system, it is important to consider the major challenges met eventually to have a system of twenty stations operating in three oceans. Further, there was responsibility for disseminating the collected data on a time-urgent basis to a number of addressees. Incorporating technological improvements and upgrading presented significant demands on the system providers and operators. Managing a fleet of seagoing cable-laying ships was another large and significant undertaking that was a part of the system.

By 1994, $16 billion had been invested for the system's construction, implementation, and operation. "At its peak, in the late 1980s, the monitoring system cost more than $300 million a year to maintain and was staffed by 2,400 officers and technicians."[5] With remission from Cold War demands in 1989, the system continues as a new tool for scientists seeking new knowledge and understanding of the ocean bottoms and their characteristics. New applications for the system include gaining knowledge relevant to global warming as well as the general environmental science of the world's oceans.

Simply referring to SOSUS in a historical context as an important Cold War participant does not do justice to the vastness and global aspects of the system in its implementation and integration into the Navy's needs. Time, cost, technology improvements and personnel considerations, including military and industry participation were as enormous as its Atlantic and Pacific Ocean coverage. The high security classification of the system always provided further demands on all concerned.

Initial interest in this surveillance concept stemmed from the improvements occurring in the Soviet submarines by their post World War II (WWII) acquisition of German submarine expertise. These Soviet submarine improvements necessitated countermeasures. Sound surveillance became an excellent countermeasure. As the Cold War progressed, Soviet submarines became quieter and the bar for surveillance was raised. With regard to the Cold War, the United States and Soviet submarines operated on a war footing in a time of peace. The role of SOSUS was a key element in countering the enemy submarines.

Similarly, the technical origins of the concept are of interest in viewing the logic of how and why SOSUS evolved. The significant way in which the system grew and improved should not be overlooked when reviewing the history.

Of the many participants in the evolution of SOSUS, it is essential that particular consideration be given to Navy Captain Charles Paul Kelly's important role, as Project Engineer from the earliest days of the system implementation until 1973.

A 1968 accounting of the number of Soviet submarines by Jane's Defensive Ships in 1968 lists 55 nuclear and 325 conventionally powered. About this time, there was awareness of Soviet submarines with depth capability of 1000 feet or greater and speed of 40 knots underwater. An operational SOSUS was well suited to detecting and locating the growing and improving Soviet submarines as a threat to the United States as they extended their operating areas It has been noted that "in the new age of nuclear propulsion both the United States and the Soviet Union had studded the ocean bottom with networks of sensors and hydrophones in a technological race to render the oceans transparent, to "bug" the seaways and gain advantage in the silent war."[7]

Before 1950: A Sound Pipeline

On October 17, 1937, geophysics professor Maurice Ewing from Lehigh University joined Columbus Iselin, then Physical Oceanographer at Woods Hole, aboard the Woods

Hole Oceanographic Institute *Atlantis* for a test cruise. Ewing conducted seismic refraction experiments to determine the thickness and makeup of sediments at the ocean bottom at depths of three miles in the North Atlantic.

Underwater explosives (10-pound TNT blocks) were used as sound source, and it was noted that a chain of echoes were generated by repeated reflections between the ocean bottom and the sea surface especially at the lower frequencies and traveled long distance underwater with limited loss. Further, if hydrophones were carefully located in this <u>deep sound channel</u>, the signals could be detected. Important implementation of this channel identification followed but not immediately.

During World War II in 1942, Maurice Ewing with J. L. Worzel at WHOI resumed work on "deep sound channel" signal propagation proposed by Ewing in 1937. Ewing theorized that low-frequency waves, which are less vulnerable than those of higher frequencies to scattering and absorption, should be able to travel great distances if the sound source is placed correctly. In analyzing the results of this test, they discovered a kind of sound pipeline, which they called he Sound Fixing and Ranging (SOFAR) channel, also known as the "deep sound channel."

An additional test was conducted in the spring of 1944 aboard the research vessel *R/V Saluda* operating in the vicinity of Eleuthera in the Bahamas. A deep-receiving <u>hydrophone</u> was hung from *R/V Saluda*. A Navy ship dropped 4-pound explosive charges set to explode at 4000 feet in the ocean at distances up to 900 miles from *R/V Saluda's* hydrophone. The Navy ship's operations were limited to this distance. Receivers located in Dakar on the west coast of Africa easily detected the underwater explosions at a range of the order of 2000 miles. Ewing and Worzel heard, for the first time, the characteristic sound of a

SOFAR transmission, consisting of a series of pulses building up to its climax.

In 1943, an application of Ewing's deep sound channel involved setting up coastal hydrophones to listen for the sound bursts from small explosives set off by pilots downed at sea while floating on life rafts to provide bearings for their location and retrieval. At that time, having a small TNT charge in conjunction with high-test aviation gasoline was deemed dangerous. In 1947, SOFAR was developed further and Pacific listening stations were established.

Concurrently, Ewing tried to get the Navy to use the deep sound channel to locate and summon help for a submarine under enemy attack. This was not pursued due to difficult coding problems.[8] Later, Ewing's deep-water channel discovery provided a basis for the mid-century Sound Surveillance System (SOSUS).

Peace in 1945 did not end the Navy's requirements for further information about the seas. Shortly after several years of an uneasy peace, international politics and technological innovations applicable to ships, submarines, aircraft, and weapons collectively brought additional high priority ocean-related Navy needs.

Encouragement to continue advancing ASW tactics and systems was stimulated when the details of German submarine developments became known near the end of the war. In the early postwar period, two Type XXI submarines became available to American, British, and Soviet navies. Increased underwater submarine speed (17 knots for up to 30 minutes), and the snorkel provided new challenges with oceanographic implications. Interest in submarine operating depths of 1000 feet also became a consideration. These technology advances strongly influenced submarine design and affirmed the importance of ASW.[9]

The new Office of Naval Research (ONR) established in August 1946 and the National Science Foundation (NSF) created in 1950 by an Act of Congress provided an environment for the support of science in the United States. At first, ONR was the principal supporter of fundamental research by U.S. scientists. Success of federally- sponsored research was partly due to government-university-industry relationships brought about by ONR.

Ewing, by then a professor at Columbia University, found support in 1946 at ONR to continue research on the deep sound channel in Bermuda. The research site was called the Navy SOFAR Station. The initial installation consisted of a hydrophone on the bottom at 800 fathoms and connected to the shore by a submarine cable.

Committee on Undersea Warfare (CUW)

In November 1945, Gaylord P. Harnwell, director of the California University of War Research Laboratory ASW and pro-submarine research at San Diego, wrote a letter to Admiral Harold Bowen, then head of the Navy Office of Research and Invention, soon to be head of the Office of Naval Research (ONR). Harnwell called for an undersea warfare committee to "maintain Naval liaison, determine membership, organize and conduct symposia, issue bulletins and summaries of proceedings."[10]

Support for Antisubmarine Warfare (ASW) research came in January 1946. Admiral Chester A. Nimitz, Chief of Naval Operations, reported to Secretary of the Navy James Forrestal that advances in submarine design and operating capability necessitated improvements in submarine detection and location systems.

A September 1946 proposal to Admiral Bowen, now head of ONR, recommended establishing a permanent

Committee on Undersea Warfare (CUW). The new committee, established October 23, 1946, reported directly to the executive board of the National Research Council (NRC), the active arm of the National Academy of Sciences (NAS). The NAS established the CUW and provided the committee with a broad pro-and anti-submarine mandate. The committee's charter allowed direct access with the executive board of the NRC, ONR, and Navy bureaus.[11]

The environment during these years focused on the antisubmarine problem from the viewpoint of the German Type XXI submarine performance and snorkel mentioned above. Soviet submarine buildup using advanced German submarine technology was a continuing threat.

Attention to Deep Channel Propagation 1949

Submarine Development Groups 1, 2

An important Navy response to the threat occurred in January 1949, when the Chief of Naval Operations (CNO) directed that "Fleet Commanders assign one division in each fleet to the sole task of solving the problem of using submarines to detect and destroy enemy submarines. All other operations of any nature even type training, ASW services or fleet tactics shall be subordinated to this mission. To this end, two Submarine Development Groups were established: Group 1 in San Diego and Group 2 in New London at the Submarine Base. Investigation of the propagation characteristics of low frequencies was an early assignment. Group 2 at New London was tasked with "solving the problem of using submarines to detect and destroy enemy submarines."[12] [13] Gradually Group 2's activities and mission expanded, and in the late 1970s it became Submarine Development Squadron Twelve.

With their assigned submarines, the Development Groups immediately initiated efforts to learn more about passive detection of submarines and submarine acoustic signatures. Further attention to deep channel propagation came from Naval Research Laboratory SOFAR tests off Point Sur, California. Using SOFAR hydrophones, submarine detection ranges of 10-15 nautical miles were reported. The above-mentioned Bermuda SOFAR installation provided additional information regarding passive detection. The experience from these SOFAR sites provided knowledge for hardware associated with shore-based detection of sounds in the ocean.[14] [15] [16]

In May 1949, at the request of Submarine Development Group 2 in New London, the work at the Bermuda SOFAR station included making acoustic signatures of fleet type submarines and snorkel-equipped submarines. Enemy submarine acoustic signatures would play an increasing important role in the evolving surveillance system. Submarine detection ranges were made from about two miles to 100 miles.[17] There was additional interest in SOFAR related to determining missile impact locations.

1950 Undersea Surveillance Support

Additional encouragement to pursue new antisubmarine research and development directions came from an April 1950 report (commissioned in 1949), Studies of Undersea Warfare by Deputy Chief of Naval Operations (CNO) Rear Admiral F. S. Low and referred to as the Low Report. A 1984 comment by Willem Hackman in Seek and Strike noted the Low Report as bringing attention to priorities for future research and development with awareness of the forthcoming nuclear submarine and long-range torpedoes.[18]

Further incentive to consider use of Ewing's sound channel at low frequencies (30 –150 Hz) resulted from the CUW Fifth Undersea Symposium held in Washington on 15 and 16 May. Frederick Hunt, director of the Harvard Underwater Sound Laboratory during WWII, presented a paper favoring the use of the sound channel for long-range signal detection. The period from the start of the Korean War June 1950 to the armistice July 27, 1953 provided additional attention to defense issues and planning.

Project Hartwell

All the above undersea warfare activities brought about a wide-ranging study in 1950 at MIT by the CUW.

The participants included well-known scientists and engineers from Bell Laboratories, California Institute of Technology, Carnegie Institution, Harvard, MIT, Marine Physical Laboratory, and the Scripps Oceanographic Institution. The comprehensive study called, Project Hartwell, addressed long-range defense against submarines.

For three months ending August 31, 1950, the group studied wide-ranging Navy problems related to the various aspects of overseas transport in a possibly unfriendly environment. This period also saw an expanding Korean War and with its requirements. The September 1950 Project Hartwell report suggested and recommended an extensive number of important measures to be pursued. It was intended that most of the Hartwell recommendations with adequate support could begin to be in service in two years. Significant effort by the Hartwell group was directed at protecting shipping against submarines and mines.[19] Regarding undersea surveillance, the Hartwell report findings included an immediate start of research to exploit the potential of low-frequency bottomed hydrophone arrays with multiple sites for triangulation to detect, identify, and track distant enemy submarines.

The Hartwell participants understood that there were unknown factors related to undersea surveillance and recommended an annual $10 million to develop an effective, long-range acoustic detection sensor system using bottomed hydrophone arrays. What would become a two-ocean surveillance system was gradually implemented. Commitment to what became SOSUS assured the Navy's continuing, strong, and growing interest in oceanography. This system concept, because of its method of operation and locations, proffered resistance to destruction, foul weather, and ambient self-generated noise features not available at the time to other surveillance technologies.

American Telephone and Telephone Company (AT&T)

During 1949, the Navy's ASW priorities regarding the enemy submarine threat were brought to the attention of industry. Dr. Mervin Kelly, then president of the Bell Telephone Laboratories of AT&T, met with CNO to discuss antisubmarine warfare. In October 1950 after the completion of Project Hartwell and its approval of quickly initiating steps to develop adequate ocean surveillance, Dr. Kelly offered the services of Bell Laboratories to the CNO.

In late December 1950, as a result of Dr. Kelly's offer, ONR contracted with Western Electric, the engineering and manufacturing part of AT&T. The $1 million research and development contract, sponsored by ONR and Bureau of Ships (Buships), was to develop an undersea surveillance system based on long-range low frequency sound propagation.

The overall effort evolved into several areas including: system design, engineering, deployment, shore station construction, hydrophone cable laying and the oceanographic research needed to understand long-range sound transmission in the sea. Caesar was the unclassified designation for the installation and production efforts. The research and development work by AT&T was designated Jezebel.

Commitment to undersea surveillance made it mandatory to broadly investigate propagation of sound in the sea and find answers to bathymetric questions such as depth and ocean contours. This part of the system development, called Michael, was under the purview of Columbia University Hudson Laboratories, Woods Hole Oceanographic Institute, Scripps Oceanographic Institute (SOI), and the Navy Hydrographic Office.

LOFAR (Low Frequency Analyzer and Recorder)

This device coming from the AT&T Bell Laboratory (BTL) became an important system component early in the surveillance program with the first unit delivered in May 1951. AT&T adapted its recently-invented sound spectrograph, a tool for analyzing speech sounds, to analyze low-frequency underwater signals in near-real time. The output of LOFAR showed on paper readout the frequency of the signals picked up by the bottomed hydrophone arrays. Through the years that the system was in use, appropriate new technologies were invoked and provided significant system performance enhancement. As more SOSUS stations were placed in operation, a vast number of LOFAR analyzer/recorders were needed to accommodate the increasing number of hydrophones. Comments regarding the personnel needed to operate these stations and their unique abilities and equipment will be addressed later. Additional appreciation for the effectiveness of the LOFAR equipment was recognized as it was introduced to the Navy's long-range maritime patrol craft (VP) and submarine communities.[20]

First Test: Sandy Hook, New Jersey

This consisted of a series of experimental trials by the installation of undersea listening arrays off Sandy Hook, NJ. (Undersea Warfare) The experiment consisted of a cable and a few hydrophones installed in shallow water with the cable terminated in a building owned by the U. S. Army. Even with the high ambient noise due to the proximity to New York Harbor, range tests demonstrated the feasibility of surveillance and submarine detection.

Captain Joseph P. Kelly, USN

In May 1951 with the ongoing Korean War Lieutenant Kelly, a WWII naval officer and member of the Naval Reserve, was recalled and reported for duty in Washington. His prior experience included working at Westinghouse in Pittsburgh as an electrical engineer on large turbine generators and cable transmission systems from 1937 to 1942, when he was commissioned as an Ensign. His WWII experience included assignment as Maintenance Officer for magnetic loops and harbor defense mine fields in Panama. At the end of WWII, he continued his work at Westinghouse.

In December 1951, he was interviewed by Rear Admiral Homer N. Wallen, Chief of the Bureau of Ships, who asked him, "What do you know about Jezebel?" His response was "What's that?" the Admiral replied, "Welcome Aboard: you're the new Project Officer." This was the beginning of Joseph's Kelly's twenty-one year association with Oceanographic surveillance.[21]

As SOSUS project manager, his diligent and unceasing efforts for more than two decades brought the nearly-global system to full operational status. Ultimately, system locations included the Atlantic and Gulf coast of the United States under the Caesar project. This was followed by surveillance covering the United States Pacific shelf from Vancouver to Baja California. Two arrays covered Soviet submarine Atlantic entry from northern Europe. Access for Soviet submarines from eastern Siberia was monitored with arrays from the southeastern tip of Japan, eastward parallel to the Kuriles and northeastern to the Aleutian Islands.[22]

Test Site: Eleuthera, Bahamas

Lieutenant Kelly, as Buships Code 849 assigned to oversee the high priority project Jezebel, obtained permission from the British government to make a surveillance installation on the island of Eleuthera in the Bahamas. With assistance from a British cable layer, underwater cable and six hydrophones were installed, three in 40 feet of water, two at 960 feet, and one at 1000 feet and in addition, the first deep-water array with a 40 hydrophone linear array (1000 feet long at 240 fathoms). The long array maximized the signal gain at the low frequencies of interest. Narrow band signal analysis maximized processing gain. With the shore-based equipment in place, the system was operational by January 1952.

A Decisive Test

On April 29, 1952, scientists from Bell Laboratories demonstrated their LOFAR passive detection system to a group of flag officers at Eleuthera. A U.S. snorkel- equipped submarine acting as a target maneuvered offshore and was given instructions to change course, speed, and depth. Final instructions required the submarine to open range and make a box maneuver every 25 miles to provide checkpoints. Positive detections of the submarine were achieved and paper output from the LOFAR (Lofargrams) convinced those present that the detections were real. In Washington steps were taken to make Project Caesar happen. In 1952, Joseph Kelly was appointed Lieutenant Commander.

Endnotes

1 Owen R. Cote, Jr., "The Third Battle: Innovation in the U. S. Navy's Silent Cold War Struggle with the Soviet Union", Naval War College, Newport, Paper Number Sixteen, 2003, p. 18.

2 Kenneth Sewell and Clint Richmond, *Red Star Rogue,* Simon & Schuster, NY, 2005, p 68, 109; New York Times, "Anti-Sub Seabed Grid Thrown Open to Research Uses," July 21, 1996, p. C1.

3 Joel S. Wit, "Advances in Antisubmarine Warfare," *Scientific American,* February 1981, Vol. 244, No. 2, p. 32.

4 William E. Burrows, *Deep Black: Space Espionage and National Security*, Random House, NY, 1986, p. 180.

5 New York Times, *op. cit.,* p. C1

6 Gary E. Weir and Walter J. Boyne, Rising Tide: *The Untold Story of the Russian Submarines that Fought the Cold War*, Basic Books, NY, 2003, p. 169.

7 Patrick Tyler, Running Critical: *The Silent War, Rickover, and General Dynamics*, Harper & Row, NY, 1986, p. 26.

8 Joe Worzel, Letter to Lamont-Doherty Earth, January 2004, Alumni Association at the Lamont-Doherty Earth Observatory. http://www.ldeo.columbia.edu/ldeo/alum/assoc/pgi.html.

9 Cote, *op. cit.,* p. 11.

10 Gary Weir, *An Ocean in Common: American Naval Officers, Scientists, and their Ocean Environment*, Texas A&M University Press, College Station TX, 2001, p. 226.

11 *Ibid,* p. 227.

12 Frank Andrews, "My View—Submarine Development Group Two," http://www.applmath.com/csds50/pdfs/MyViewSub.pdf ; United States Navy Submarine Development Group Two and Submarine Development Squadron Twelve A Royal Navy Exchange Perspective 1955 to Date (2003), compiled by Captain D. W. Mitchell Royal March 2003.

13 Cote, *op. cit.,* p. 14.

14 Sound Ocean Surveillance System: The Origins of SOSUS, Space and Naval Warfare Systems document, http://web. Archive.org/web/2000012207553/http://www/Spawar.navy.mil/co mmands/co…

15 Gordon R. Hamilton, Reminiscences about Early Lamont, http://www.ldeo.columbia.edu/ideo/alum/stories/Hamilton_Gordon _Reminiscences-2.htm

16 Worzel, *op. cit.,* p. 3.

17 ibid.

18 Willem Hackmann, *Seek & Strike: Sonar, anti-submarine warfare and the Royal Navy 1914-54*, London, Her Majesty's Stationery Office, 1984, p. 341.

19 Project Hartwell, http://handle.dtic.mil/100.2/ADA800012

20 Cote, *op. cit.,* p. 34.

21 "Captain Joseph Kelly, Commander, Undersea Warfare: Father of SOSUS," http://www.cus.navy.mil/kelly.htm

22 Jeffrey T. Richelson, *The U.S. Intelligence Community,* Westview Press, Boulder, CO, 1999, p. 232-335.

Remembering:

The Sound Surveillance System (SOSUS)

Part II

Caesar First Steps

In June 1952, with the successful LOFAR detection of submarines at Sandy Hook and Eleuthera and long experience with SOFAR, the Chief of Naval Operations (CNO) directed Bureau of Ships to acquire six stations under CAESAR, increasing to nine stations in September. Three contracts were implemented to include equipment, installation, and construction or expansion of a cable-manufacturing facility. The Simplex Wire and Cable Company in New England was expanded to manufacture the miles of cables needed for Caesar installations.

In a 1952 letter to CNO, the Commander in Chief of the Pacific Fleet indicated interest in the system and offered suggestions regarding Pacific Ocean locations for future sites. By May 1954, ten more stations were planned with six on the West Coast. An unclassified cover story was created for the new system and the low frequency passive detection development was designated SOSUS.

During the next five years, SOSUS facilities were installed and commissioned along the eastern Atlantic Ocean. "They form a huge semicircle from Barbados to Nova Scotia, opening toward the deepwater abyss west of the mid-Atlantic Ridge. This provided both excellent coverage of the deep ocean basin off the eastern seaboard and the opportunity for contact correlation among arrays with widely separated vantage points."[23]

Likely Soviet submarine routes to gain access to the United States eastern seaboard provided a basis for the location of SOSUS hydrophone arrays.[24] The results of Lt. Cmdr. Joseph Kelly's efforts during the first years of the project are shown in the table.

Caesar Cable Fleet Ships

WHOI, SOI, and Columbia University's Hudson Laboratory under Project Michael dealt with finding answers to questions regarding cable placement. The Navy cable ships and AT&T accomplished the actual laying of the hundreds of miles of cables in depths up to 1000 fathoms. Initially the cable ships Neptune and Myer were assigned. Later, ships Thor, Aeolus, Mizar, Huddell, Zeus and USNS Waters made up the cable fleet. They became known as the Caesar Fleet. Some locations where deep water was available needed ten or twenty miles of cable while others required a hundred miles. At some point in the SOSUS years, 30,000 miles of undersea cable and more than 1000 hydrophones were maintained.[25][26]

NAVFACS

The shore station facilities located along the coasts with their hydrophone arrays, buildings, and instrumentation came to be identified as NAVFACS. Sites were chosen where the continental shelf break came closest to land. Upon the completion of the installation and in operation, sufficient manpower for the daily 24-hour operation placed a requirement of 100 or more personnel at each facility. The unique skills for reading and interpreting the LOFAR analyzer's black and grey paper printout made training and education important requirements.

The number of LOFAR analyzers at each NAVFAC was quite large "A Lofar analyzer was associated with each beam of each array served by a NAVFAC, and typically, the large watch floors were filled with hundreds of these "gram-writers: busily turning out Lofargrams on 'smoky paper 24 hours a day.'"[27]   Equipment maintenance, data collection and its transfer to centers for analysis and operational commands provided continuing challenges. Eventually more than twenty stations were in operation and met a manpower requirement of several thousand.

Project Caesar Stations Commissioned 1954-59

1954 Ramey, Puerto Rico-Grand Turk-San Salvador

1955 Bermuda, Shelburne, Nova Scotia, Nantucket, MA, Cape May, NJ

1956 Cape Hatteras, NC, Antigua

1958 Point Sur, CA, Centerville Beach, CA, Pacific Beach, WA, Coos Head, OR, Argentia, Newfoundland

Continuing SOSUS Expansion and Operational Example

With the above clusters of stations in 1956 and more to follow, the concept of regional SOSUS Evaluation Centers was adopted to correlate contact information and provide reacquisition data concerning the target for use by patrol aircraft, surface ships and submarines. Later, the Centers were called Naval Oceanographic Processing Facilities (NOPFs). The first two were in Norfolk and New York. Combined with other intelligence, the resulting target position estimates and probability areas were provided to local and regional ASW commands.[28]

At the end of the 1950s, "SOSUS cables and hydrophones, separated by intervals of five to fifteen miles, were also laid off Denmark, Iceland, Norway, the North Cape, Italy, Spain, Turkey, and around the British Isles."[29]

Expansion of SOSUS stations was modest in 1961 with one NAVFAC placed in operation at Adak, Alaska, not far from the western tip of that state. On the operational side, as a demonstration, East Coast United States SOSUS arrays successfully tracked the first Fleet Ballistic Missile submarine, the USS George Washington (SSN 598) on its first transit from the United States across the North Atlantic to the United Kingdom.

1962 Soviet Submarines and SOSUS

The Cuban Missile Crisis (July-November 1962), provided opportunity for the Atlantic SOSUS stations to have an important role in the naval blockade. The heightened time was during October. In June, the SOSUS NAVFAC at Cape Hatteras identified the first Soviet diesel. The following month, NAVFAC Barbados made the first detection by SOSUS of a Soviet Nuclear submarine as it crossed the Greenland-Iceland-UK gap. "…

SOSUS was able to exploit the fact that both propellers and rotating machinery mounted directly to a submarine's hull generated, predictable narrowband tonals at source levels high enough for large LOFAR arrays to detect them and track them on an ocean wide basis."[30] From SOSUS data, Neptune naval aircraft (P-24) were able to broadcast in the clear the exact locations of Soviet Submarines and were heard by the Soviet submarines as well as blockade members.[31] ASW aircraft, in addition to the cueing advantage by the long range SOSUS detection data, were further enhanced by the use of their aircraft launched sonobuoys in the pursuit of the Soviet submarines.

During October at the peak of the crisis, Soviet Foxtrot submarines (nuclear torpedo equipped), in transit to and in the Cuban area were detected by SOSUS and closely trailed). The tracking data was passed to the Navy blockade participants. After the crisis was resolved, the observed SOSUS effectiveness led to the expansion and upgrading of the network. A SOSUS array was placed to cover the Greenland-Iceland-United Kingdom (GIUK) Gap with NAVFAC Keflavik established in 1966. One path for Soviet

Submarines to the Atlantic and the United States from the northern Soviet submarine base was through the Gap.[32]

Data from these widely-distributed arrays brought attention to new uses for the underwater surveillance. In 1965-66, the Norway SOSUS array detected and tracked Soviet Bear-D bombers flying over the Norwegian Sea. Surface ship detection as well as detection of nuclear explosions occurring near oceans or underwater was included in SOSUS capability. With 55 Soviet nuclear submarines deployed between 1958 and 1968, opportunities for SOSUS detection were increased.[33]

1962 USS Thresher (SSN 593)

On Sunday April 9, 1963, the Thresher was lost with all hands at a depth of 8400 feet 260 miles off the New England coast. Nearby oceanographic ships and others were able to identify an area of interest. A chronology of SOSUS for the year of the tragedy cites "SOSUS plays critical role in pinpointing the location of the incident."

Strong interest in determining the cause of the submarine loss was directed at the obvious to prevent future similar events. In this regard, resolution of the question of whether the loss might be due to deliberate enemy action was critical.[34] Was the loss from an explosion or implosion? The Navy's Deep Submergence Rescue Vehicle (DSRV) development was one of the results of the loss of the Thresher.

1968: Soviet K-129

In 1968, SOSUS Pacific operations included a new operational NAVFAC at Midway Island and the commissioning of the Guam, Mariana Islands NAVFAC. First SOSUS detections of Victor and Charlie Class Soviet nuclear submarines occurred at the Keflavik, Iceland station.[35]

SOSUS involvement occurred with the April loss of the Soviet ballistic missile, first Soviet submarine with underwater launch, diesel electric Golf (K-129) submarine in the Pacific northwest of Hawaii and a few weeks later on May 27 with the loss of the USS Scorpion (SSN 589) in the Atlantic in water with depths of the order of 15,000 feet.[36]

The mid-Pacific SOSUS array (code-name Sea Spider: a 1,300-mile-long circular array surrounding the Hawaiian Islands) has been cited as the array that monitored and localized the breakup of the Soviet submarine K-129.[37]

In both submarine losses, sound surveillance data contributed to the overall effort to determine the location of each lost submarine. The United States search for the Scorpion was undertaken with reasonable public exposure while the Soviet search was extremely classified. The United States search for the K-129 included careful security measures. Searching for the submarines at great depths and, in the case of the Pacific location, of the order of 15,000 feet or greater made the searches extremely difficult and complex. Developing accurate information concerning the reasons for the losses provided a broad number of challenges.

USS Scorpion (SSN 589)

Regarding the Scorpion loss on a return trip to the United States, it was realized that during a three thousand mile track from southern Europe, the sounds of its collapse and the implosions at collapse depth might have been recorded. A Naval Research Laboratory (NRL) research station in the Canary Islands equipped with a hydrophone found about five separate trains of acoustic events that could have been associated with a submarine breakup.

In addition, "Kelly (now a Captain) came to the rescue with his awareness of a super-secret hydrophone installations in the hands of another government agency. The sounds of Scorpion's death might be buried in this organization."[38] Captain Kelly's resourcefulness led to additional Scorpion acoustic signatures. Collectively the signatures and using triangulation identified a location for the Scorpion. The following year, the deep submergence vehicle Trieste II provided further details of the Scorpion's sinking. The Scorpion was 400 miles southwest of the Azores at 10,000 feet.

Continuing interest in the Scorpion recently in the 2006 book "Silent Steel" brings further revelations regarding the search for the submarine.[39] The author points out that it was the additional acoustic signal picked up by the Air Force's Technical Applications Center (AFTAC) facility in Argentia, Newfoundland. The facility's purpose was monitoring Soviet nuclear weapon tests. AFTAC's implosion data coupled acoustic data from the SOFAR operation on La Palma, a small island in the Canary Islands that identified the submarine's location.

High point

Under Captain Joseph Kelly, SOSUS grew in size, improved its operations and methods, and more than met its purpose. At the time of his retirement in April 1973 after more than 20 years as SOSUS Project Manager, there were a total of 22 SOSUS installations along the East and West Coasts of the United States.

SOSUS success in the 1970s and the availability of effective air-dropped homing torpedoes and more intensive use of the P3 Orion patrol squadrons allowed the U.S. submarines to withdraw from earlier Cold War stations off Soviet coastal waters and to adopt instead a barrier strategy in the Norwegian Seas, along the Greenland-United Kingdom line, and at chokepoints in the North Pacific.[40] In summary, "By 1981, unclassified depictions of SOSUS described it as having 36 installations, including facilities located in Continental United States (CONUS), the United Kingdom, Turkey, Japan, the Aleutians, Hawaii, Puerto Rico, Bermuda. Barbados, Canada, Norway, Iceland, the Azores, Italy, Denmark, Gibraltar, the Ryukyus, Panama, the Philippines, Guam, and Diego Garcia."[41]

SOSUS Eclipsed

The mid-1980s brought several technology changes that challenged SOSUS's role. The Soviet submarine ballistic missile range changed from the early days of SOSUS. The Soviet initial range of 350-1600 nautical miles (nm) increased to ranges of the order of 4900 nm. This enhancement placed Soviet ballistic missile submarines closer to the USSR, typically further from SOSUS locations.[42] Soviet SSBNs no longer needed to pass through the SOSUS barriers to reach their targets. Soviet SSBN patrols could be conducted in the marginal ice seas of the Soviet Arctic littoral, including the Norwegian and Barents Seas and later under the permanent ice of the Arctic Ocean, and be provided with support by the rest of the Soviet Navy.[43] SOSUS was beginning to be perceived as an aging system and not capable of covering large mid-ocean areas.[44]

During the period 1967 to 1985, John A. Walker, a U.S. Navy warrant officer and career submarine communication expert watch officer in Norfolk, VA, continuously shared submarine information with the Soviets until 1976 when he retired and afterwards. In 1985, he was taken into custody. Soviet knowledge of SOSUS success contributed to the rapid quieting of Soviet submarines, making them more difficult noise sources to detect and localize.

Towed Sonar Arrays

In the late 1960s, there was significant and growing interest in the use of towed sonar arrays for ASW. As a result, by September 1970 systems were installed on three Dealey class destroyers in the Mediterranean. Demonstrations of these arrays were eminently successful. "During their stay in the Mediterranean, they accounted for over 50% of all submarine detections by any method, including visual sighting."[45]

The comments of Rear Admiral J. R. Hill, RN, regarding towed arrays in a 1984 assessment of ASW was one of the many statements that emphasized the significance of towed array development. "The passive sonar towed array...may well be the most important single development in ASW sensors since 1945."[46]

Surveillance Towed Array Sensor System (SURTASS)

Gradually quieter Soviet submarines of the 1960s and 1970s created a need for mobile towed array detection. In the mid-1970s, the Navy contracted with the Hughes Aircraft Company to develop the equipment for mobile surface ship detection. The latest computer technology for the computer-based sonar was expensive and required long development time. As a fixed system, SOSUS presented a wartime target and restriction to operate in certain areas. With its mobility SURTASS complemented SOSUS. Further enhancement for the undersea surveillance came from active and passive sonobuoys.[47]

Ships

Towed array ships required special design to accommodate the equipment, long arrays and extended patrols. In 1984, the first SURTASS ship of 18 United States Navy Ships for the Hughes developed equipment and arrays was commissioned. It was a mono-hull design and manned with a civilian and military crew. The ships are 224 feet long, beam of 43 foot-beam displacing 2,262 tons, with a speed of 11 knots, and capable of ASW patrols of 60-90 days.[48] SURTASS ships require stability at low speeds and in rough waters.[49]

The towed linear array of 8575 feet was deployed on a 6000 ft neutrally-buoyant cable. SURTASS ships are manned with civilian mariners under contract to the Military Sealift Command and are designated United States Naval Ships (USNS). Ports of operation include Glasgow Scotland; Rota, Spain; Yokohama, Japan; Pearl Harbor, Hawaii; and Port Hueneme, California. At this time, SURTASS joined SOSUS, and the combined name for these two systems became the Integrated Undersea Surveillance System (IUSS).

SURTASS vessels send, via satellite, the gathered data on ocean sound signals and other target information to East and West Coast shore-based processing stations for transmittal to numbered fleets. These ships improved the Navy's ability to locate Soviet submarines and monitor their fleet bases, but a wartime environment would restrict them to deep ocean areas.[50]

End of Cold War and New SOSUS Users

The official date for the end of the Cold War, December 26, 1991, brought a lessening of the need for SOSUS, and the system mission was declassified after forty-one years of secrecy. That year, Federal scientists in Newport, OR began to use SOSUS to listen to seaquakes, quickly detecting thousands of them. In 1993, the scientists monitored the explosive fury of a deep-sea volcanic eruption and sent a small flotilla of research ships, robots, and submersibles to explore the site.

SOSUS BUDGET	
Year	Amount (million)
1991	$335
1994	$165
1995	$ 60 (estimate)

The status of SOSUS is reflected in the budget table. A steady reduction occurred in the manpower assignments with 2500 for 1993, 2000 for 1994, and 750 for 1996. SURTASS technology and the end of the Cold War eclipsed SOSUS's position. It diminished the need for global surveillance while the SURTASS technology offered mid-ocean coverage and mobility.

New uses for SOSUS began. In 1992, the Navy, the National Marine Fisheries Service and the Coast Guard used SOSUS to track fishing vessels in the Pacific to explore possible enforcement of international bans on drift-net fishing. Over a two-year period (1992-93), biologists used SOSUS to track the migrations of whales including a single blue whale as it swam southward from Cape Cod to Bermuda to Florida and back to Bermuda. All told, for about 1700 miles it was closely monitored.[51]

To accommodate downsizing, SOSUS hydrophone arrays in both the Atlantic and Pacific became involved in shutdowns and closings. To reduce manpower requirements and realize other efficiencies, most of the original arrays were re-terminated at alternative shore sites or remoted to central processing facilities that allowed a reduction in the number of operational NAFACs. These transitions were completed in 1997 and 1998.

As mentioned previously, IUSS (formed in the mid-1980s to bring SOSUS and SURTASS under one head) is made up of fixed, mobile, and deployable acoustic arrays that provide vital tactical cueing to ASW forces. It is the Navy's primary means of submarine detection, both nuclear and diesel, continuing as an effective force multiplier, and in the post-Cold War period provides mobile detection, tracking, and reporting of submarine contacts at long range.[52] IUSS claims more contact holding hours since 1997 than all other anti-submarine warfare (ASW) platforms combined.

Endnotes

[23] Edward C. Whitman, "First Generation Installations and Initial Operational Experience (SOSUS)," Undersea Warfare, Winter 2005, Vol. 7, No. 2, p. 1.

[24] Gary E. Weir and Walter J. Boyne, <u>Rising Tide</u>: *The Untold Story of the Russian Submarines that Fought the Cold War*, Basic Books, NY, 2003, p. 114.

[25] SOSUS – Archived 12/2005, p. 3.
http://www.forecastinternational.com/archive/c3/c34622.htm.

[26] "Scientists Oppose Navy Plan to Close Undersea System," <u>The Virginian Pilot</u>, June 12, 1994

[27] C:\Documents and Settings\User\My Documents\SOSUS\EagleSpeak Sunday Ship History U.S. Navy Cable Repair Ships.mht.

[28] Edward C. Whitman, "First Generation Installations and Initial Operational Experience (SOSUS)," Undersea Warfare, Winter 2005, Vol. 7, No. 2, p. 1.

[29] Robert W. Love Jr., *History of the U. S. Navy: Vol. Two, 1942-1991*, Stackpole Books, Harrisburg, PA 17105, 1992, p. 387.

[30] Owen R. Cote, Jr., "The Third Battle: Innovation in the U. S. Navy's Silent Cold War Struggle with the Soviet Union," Naval War College, Newport, Paper Number Sixteen, 2003, p. 34.

[31] Gary Weir and Walter Boyne, *op. cit.,* p. 91.

[32] Jeffrey T. Richelson, *The U.S. Intelligence Community,* Westview Press Boulder, CO, 1999, p. 233.

[33] Cote, *op. cit.,* p. 64.

[34] John Pina Craven, *The Silent War: The Cold War Battle Beneath the Sea,* Simon& Schuster, NY, 2001, p. 106.

[35] Whitman, *op. cit.,* p. 1.

[36] Gary Weir and Walter Boyne, *op. cit.,* p. 110.

[37] Richelson, *op. cit.,* p. 233.

[38] Craven, *op. cit.,* p. 203.

[39] Stephen Johnson, *Silent Steel,* Wiley publisher, NY, 2006, p. 130.

[40] Love, *op. cit.,* p. 612.

[41] Owen R. Cote, Jr., *op. cit.,* p. 36.

[42] Jeffrey T. Richelson, *op. cit.,* p. 234.

[43] Cote, *op. cit.,* p. 54.

[44] Love, *op. cit.,* p. 712.

[45] Stanley G. Lemon, "Towed-Array History, 1917-2003," <u>IEEE Journal of Oceanic Engineering</u>, Vol. 29. No. 2. April 2004, p 368.

[46] Rear Admiral J. R. Hill, *Antisubmarine Warfare*, Annapolis, Naval Institute Press, 1984, p. 69.

[47] Willem Hackmann, *Seek & Strike: Sonar, anti-submarine warfare and the Royal Navy 1914-54*, London, Her Majesty's Stationery Office, 1984, p. 355.

[48] Whitman, *op. cit.,* p. 2.

[49] Love JR, *op. cit.,* p. 712.

[50] *ibid* p. 712-713.

[51] New York Times, June 12,1994, p. 1.

[52] John Parish et al. "An Undersea Coastal Surveillance System," Naval Submarine Review, January 1996, p. 43.